Joseph 'Tex' Geddes was born in 1919 in Peterhead, Aberdeen-shire, and is believed to have been brought up in Canada. Expelled from school at the age of 12, he tried his hand at various jobs, including boxing and rum-smuggling. During the Second World War he served with the Seaforth Highlanders and the Special Forces, and after the war became a shark fisherman, at first working with Gavin Maxwell, author of the bestselling *Ring of Bright Water*. Tex Geddes went on to purchase the tiny island of Soay, near Skye, where he lived with his wife Jeanne, continued to hunt sharks and became the Laird. He died in 1998.

Hebridean Sharker

TEX GEDDES

BIRLINN

To

JIM BORDERS
who believed I could do it

This edition first published in 2012 by
Birlinn Limited
West Newington House
10 Newington Road
Edinburgh
www.birlinn.co.uk

First published in 1960 by Herbert Jenkins Ltd, London

A CIP record for this book is available from the British Library

ISBN 978 1 78027 034 0

Designed and typeset by Hewer Text UK Ltd
Printed and bound by Clays Ltd, St Ives plc

Contents

Chapter One

This begins as most stories end: 'And so they were married and lived happily ever after.' We were married in London, at Christchurch, Ealing, just before Christmas 1948. I shall never forget the pep talk the young Canadian minister gave Jeanne and me the day before the ceremony. 'If you have any ideas that this marrying business is only to try, and if it does not work out can be dissolved, don't come here tomorrow!' Nevertheless we did arrive on the morrow, where my wife's brother, who was to give her away, met for the first time my friend, Hugh MacDonnell. He had been shipmates with me during the war in a most peculiar army then training in the Highlands, and he had come down (or up) from Scotland to act as best man and give me moral support. It was funny to see them eyeing each other, two men who had never met before, standing at the altar steps taking part in a wedding ceremony. I was amazed how quickly it was over and all that remained was the signing of the register. I had crossed my Rubicon.

Although I had spent in all eight years in the Army, self-discipline was never my strong point, probably due to my free and easy early years. To quote from Tangye, who put it so neatly when he wrote: 'They say that the average Newfoundlander just hasn't any sense of citizenship; that he is a freedom-loving individualist who is determined to do exactly as he wants according to the narrow limits of his life, and for this state of mind they blame the sea.' My life had not been devoted entirely to the sea, for strangely enough I had a great love for the Scottish Highlands, and in particular for deer and deer-stalking. Every spare moment of my time, when not

1

actually fishing, I spent in the hills with the stalkers. In retrospect I could, and most probably should, have made more money if I had stayed out of the hills, but money-making was never my aim. Suffice it to say that I liked the sea, but loved the mountains. There was nothing worthwhile to be earned deer-stalking, so I compromised and went to sea for bread and butter.

I had first met Jeanne in 1944, in Meoble, a deer forest of some 30,000 acres of mountain in the southern shore of Loch Morar in Inverness-shire. At that time Meoble Forest was one of many special training schools established in the Highlands where men from all over the world were taught sabotage and espionage. In these schools I made many friends among the gamekeepers and stalkers, and returned to live permanently in the area after my discharge.

We had arranged to spend part of our honeymoon in Meoble with Hugh's parents. This would give him the opportunity to spend a really long holiday in London free from any fear that his old father would have to manage the boats alone, for I knew Loch Morar like the back of my hand. Many a dark and stormy winter's night had Hugh and I battled our way up and down its fourteen treacherous miles, where the wind seems to gather velocity as it funnels through the mountains. There is no road to Meoble unless you climb over the mountains from Loch Ailort, and therefore everything and everyone must be ferried the nine miles from Morar.

After the formalities were over and Hugh had deafened the neighbours with his bagpipes we caught the night train for Scotland – or, to be more exact, we caught *a* night train, having missed the one on which we had our sleeper reservations. The farther north we travelled the more seasonable became the weather and when we reached Mallaig there was a blizzard of driving snow, with a full gale of wind.

We quickly installed ourselves in the West Highland Hotel where we booked a room for the night, having phoned Duncan, Hugh's father, and arranged for him to meet us at Morar pier in the morning should the weather permit. Mallaig (with the accent on the first syllable and not the last, as the lady announcer at King's Cross would have you believe) is the end of the line and the jumping-off place for the Hebrides, but it would only take us five minutes in the train to cover the three miles back to Morar.

I had been fishing out of Mallaig since I left the forces and had not told anyone where I was going or why, when I left for London, specifically to escape the ragging there invariably is when a fisherman is fool enough to admit that he is to be married.

After we had had our meal we put on our duffel coats and, braving the snow, made for the harbour and the pub, to introduce Jeanne to some of what she then referred to as 'my fishy friends'. Just as we were going into the first bar I was hailed by Dan MacGillevray, an old shipmate of mine.

'God, Tex, where have you been? I've been searching all over the village for you. Didn't you see the mustering rocket go off? Come on, there's a call for the lifeboat and you are the only member of the crew I've found so far.'

It transpired that the coxswain was out of the village and most of the regular crew had gone home for the New Year. Most of Mallaig's fishermen come of east-coast stock and they like to go 'home' as they call it, to spend the festive season with their relatives, even though they may have lived in Mallaig for twenty years.

At first I did not want to go; it was after all, in effect, my wedding night. 'Surely you can get someone to take my place tonight of all nights?' I pleaded.

Muttering under his breath, Dan hurried away to collect a crew as best he could, leaving Jeanne and me to make for the lounge bar. We didn't go in, for, as I watched his retreating figure, I was torn between my natural desire to stay and the knowledge that I ought to be at my place in the lifeboat. The idea that men might lose their lives because the boat had only an inexperienced crew on such a night haunted me. Jeanne must have read my thoughts. 'Do you want to go, Tex?' she said.

This solved my dilemma and, leaving her to go back alone to

3

the hotel, I raced down the road after Dan and caught up with him on the pier head. There we found that Jackie Kennedy, the engineer and wireless operator, had brought the lifeboat alongside the fishquay.

'How many men have you got so far, Dan?' I asked.

'Just you and me and Jackie,' Dan replied, having drawn the right conclusion from my reappearance. 'I never believed you'd let the boat sail without you!'

They quickly made up the crew from volunteers on the pier while I went and got my seaboots (the oilskins are kept in the lifeboat and today boots as well are provided by the R.N.L.I.). Jumping aboard I dressed myself in oilskins and buckled on my lifejacket. Before we were under way Jeanne had joined the crowd on the pier; she did not look particularly happy. She was hatless and, the gale having blown off the hood of her duffel coat, her long hair was flying in all directions; yet she managed a cheerful wave as we drew away from the pier.

In the entrance to Mallaig harbour there is a reef with a small automatic lighthouse on it and just as we drew abreast a huge sea broke aboard us from our port beam and flung us, I felt sure, right on to the reef; whenever that night is discussed by the boys who made up the crew, there is still argument as to whether we were on it or tossed clean over it. Anyway, we were never nearer to losing the lifeboat, and perhaps some of our lives, than we were then, and in full view of the people watching us put to sea from the pier head. Clear of the harbour we met following sea heavy enough to break over her aft and roll right forward over her nose. As bowman I had to get to my station right forward where there is a sort of bo'sun's locker, actually a small hold protected by a very strong mahogany hood. All sorts of ropes, a breeches buoy, lifelines, axes, sheath knives and a couple of oil tanks with hand pumps to calm the sea in the immediate vicinity of a wreck, are kept there. The gun for firing the lifeline is kept in the little wireless room just aft of my wee den of ropes, and I had to get down there to prepare a lifeline and check over the gun. I was wearing

4

long thigh boots and before I could get to the wireless room they were full up to the top, my legs being carried from under me several times by the weight of water which constantly broke over the boat. We are used to that and know how to hang on and, more important, where to hang on, for even the finest seaman, unless he knows his boat well enough to find handholds in the dark, is liable to go over the side. I was damn glad to get down into the wireless room and get the hatch sealed behind me, having let down half the Minch with me, at least that was how Jackie described it. Pulling off my seaboots and emptying them out, I replied that in that case a wee drop more would not hurt.

Here, in the shelter of the wireless room, I could fix up my lifelines and check over the gun, which is kept here because, with the exception of the engine room, this is the only really dry place in the boat. I intended to stay down in the wireless room until we got to the Narrows of Kyle Rhea, where I knew we would get some shelter, at least enough to make it safe to move about on deck. As I worked on the lines I was able to listen to Jackie's spasmodic bursts of conversation with Oban radio station and the radio at Erraid, but their messages appeared to be rather vague. All they were able to tell him was that a Fleetwood trawler was ashore somewhere in the vicinity of Kyle of Lochalsh and that the Kyle telephone lines were now out of order, probably blown down. We were to get there and ascertain from the Harbour Master or Coastguard where the trawler actually was.

Eventually the boat stopped her antics, having done everything but loop the loop, and I was as pleased to open the hatch as I had been to close it, for the wireless room is minute. At this juncture Jackie began to swear like a trooper.

'What's up?' I asked him.

'The bloody wireless is dead,' he replied. 'Not one cheep out of it since we entered the Narrows at Kyle Rhea.' This intelligence I brought aft, leaving Jackie to twist knobs, pull switches and curse, or whatever one does to make wireless sets work. By the time we reached Kyle he had given it up and joined us aft at the cockpit, busying himself preparing a powerful searchlight. As we drew abreast of the pier we turned the searchlight on it, and there within a couple of hundred yards of the pier head was our trawler – a great ugly, rusty bitch, high and dry and still on an even keel, mocking us, and apparently not a thing wrong with her. She had been coming in round the end of the quay to the sheltered side and had carried her way too long, or her engine had stuck in gear, and she had run ashore at the top of high water in the quietest place she could possibly have found.

All the shipwrecked mariners we had come to rescue had to do to save themselves was step off the trawler's stem almost on to the main road; to add insult to injury, these same ship-wrecked mariners caught our ropes for us when we came in alongside the pier. Dan and I at once got in touch with the station-master, whose office was about a hundred yards from the pierhead. He told us that the telephone was now in working order and that they had phoned the radio station at Oban to have us turned back. They did not require a lifeboat in the first place and had only been reporting that a trawler had overshot the pier and run aground when their telephone had gone on the bum; they also told us that Oban radio had been trying to get us all night to tell us this. You can well imagine how we felt. There we were, all soaked to the skin, having risked our necks getting there on a night of this sort and all for nothing. Of all the many occasions that I have been with the lifeboat when she has gone out to a boat reported in distress, this was the first and only time it proved a false alarm.

We were all invited aboard the *Lochmor*, one of MacBrayne's inter-island mail and passenger steamers, a squat wee ship of about 500 tons, which was lying stormbound at the pier. The late Captain Robertson was then in command. A well-known character, liked by everyone, he had a ready wit and some of his anecdotes have become almost legendary. His high, reedy voice issuing so surprisingly from his portly figure had earned him the nickname 'Squeaky', and bellowing above the wind as it shrieked through the rigging, he bade us, 'Come aboard, boys, and we'll dig out the steward. He'll find something to warm you up and the lads on watch will have a roaring fire going.'

Soon we were all grouped round the roaring fire, each with a mug of hot rum.

'Surely you're not going to batter her back to Mallaig tonight? Why not stay aboard here?' he suggested. 'It would have been bad enough running before the wind but you'll get your bellyful if you batter her back against it.'

The majority of the crew were more than willing to stay where they were, but Jackie and I were for home, and I quoted from the orders: '. . . a lifeboat on completion of a mission must return to her base with all speed, refuel, and put the boat in order for the next call.' The only man who knew about my marriage was Dan and I had asked him to say nothing.

We waited an hour or so in order to be in the Narrows at slack water, for an eight-knot current runs through there and this, added to the strength of the wind, might make a passage through impossible. It was decided that we should take turns at the wheel because on such a night, with its stinging, blinding sleet, no man could face into the wind for long. The most dangerous part of our journey home was going through the Narrows. Two miles long and only a few hundred yards wide, the towering mountains on either side turned them into a funnel for the wind, which tore at everything and screamed through the rigging, making a fearful din. When I had my first trick at the wheel I found it almost impossible to keep my eyes open; I certainly could not see the seas until they were on us, for the mountains which shut us in made the darkness seem impenetrable.

As we neared the mouth of the Narrows I realized that with that strength of wind there would be some very heavy seas piling up, but at least we would have searoom, although I had no delusions as to the hammering in store for us. As we emerged a huge sea hit us, lifting her up and up until she almost stood on end; and the engines were immediately eased to dead slow. It seemed ages before she straightened out, only to fall at once almost vertically down into the trough on the other side. The immensity of the hole we dived into made me wonder momentarily how much water remained between us and the bottom. She shook herself and began to climb out again when a terrific sea broke aboard her and for a moment or two she must have been completely submerged. The cockpit filled with water and we were up to our waists holding on for dear life, while she reared up and flung most of the water over her stern. Quite a number of such waves broke aboard us while we were down in a trough, but we just kept on going through them. I remember Jim Henderson, a Mallaig lobster fisherman who was at the wheel at that time, shouting cheerily to no one in particular: 'Over or under boys, she must go now!' and feeling sure that he was enjoying his battle with the elements, safe in the knowledge that the little boat was the best that money could buy. So long as her head kept up to the sea and her engines were eased at the right moment, to keep her from boring in too hard at the bottom of a trough, she would always come through on the other side. During this time it was quite impossible to move about on deck. Jackie was stuck in his wee wireless den and I wondered how he was getting on. Anyone who tried to leave the cockpit then would have been blown away like a feather or washed over the side like a spent match.

Clear of the Narrows the seas grew farther apart, giving us a better chance to handle the boat. I am not quite sure where we were when the sleet stopped, for there was plenty of water about all the time and we were being continuously drenched with spray. Despite this, I made my way cautiously forward to see how Jackie was making out. He was still alive, sitting on the floor with his back braced against the seat locker and his feet hard against the other, with his headphones in place over his ears, although he later admitted to taking them off during the worst of it in case he should break the cable. He was by then in touch with Oban radio and told me that there was nothing wrong with his wireless sets but, when he had entered the Narrows on the way up to Kyle, the mountains had blotted us out. He also told me that news of our position would be in Mallaig by now, for he had ordered fuel as was our normal procedure. This message was relayed to Mallaig by telephone from Oban radio. We arrived in Mallaig about 6.30 a.m. and finding the oil merchant waiting with his tanker we refuelled at once, put the boat to anchor and beat it for our respective homes.

We had each earned £1 for the first two hours at sea and 5s. an hour thereafter; in summer it would have been 15s. and 4s. thereafter.

Before leaving the lifeboat I would like to describe her, for she is no longer in Mallaig, having been replaced by a larger and faster boat. A Watson-type deep-water boat, she was forty-six feet nine inches by twelve feet nine inches with a displacement of twenty-two and a half tons. She was powered by a pair of forty hp diesels, giving her a maximum speed of eight and a quarter knots, and her fuel capacity gave her a safe range of sixty miles.

There are many different types of lifeboat, for a boat suitable for service in one coastal area may be the wrong type for another. Even so they can be roughly divided into two classes, deep- and shallow-water boats. Shallow-water boats are invariably used in areas where there are estuaries or where they have to be launched from a beach; there are no shallow-water boats in the north-west of Scotland. It has been found that a well-built boat of double-skinned diagonal planking of Honduras mahogany on straightgrained Canadian rock elm or oak frames will come through her rigorous trials better than one of steel construction, the possibly superior strength of the steel being offset by the much greater weight for equal buoyancy. It is not uncommon for a lifeboat's bottom to be damaged in service, and one or more of her holds to become flooded; this condition is not, however, serious, for not only are all the bulkheads watertight, but every available space below decks is filled with small portable wooden buoyancy tanks, each constructed to fit its own particular place in the boat. Built in this way, a lifeboat is as nearly unsinkable as a boat can be made. There has been at least one case where the hull of a lifeboat has been damaged beyond repair and yet she floated safely.

Before a new lifeboat comes into service she undergoes a series of tests; for instance, to ensure that her buoyancy tanks will keep her up, all her holds are flooded, and in this state she must not only float but be stable. In addition, the engine room is flooded to ensure that the engines will still run when completely submerged; to make this possible lifeboat's engines are so encased as to be completely watertight, but the air intakes are carried high up through the deck to the exhaust funnel. The unusual requirements imposed upon the construction of modern lifeboats by the stresses and strains inherent in their hazardous duties make them costly to build. The Mallaig lifeboat cost £12,000 when she was built in 1938, but the same type of boat today would cost £30,000. Further changes and improvements are constantly being effected: more shelter for the crew and rescued personnel; better radio communications, etc. Five international conferences have been held, the first in London in 1924, the next in Paris, a third in Holland, a fourth in Sweden and the latest in Oslo in 1947. At these conferences much has been done by interchange of ideas to improve both design and construction of the modern lifeboat.

The Royal National Lifeboat Institution came into being in 1824. Their first powered lifeboat was built in 1890, she had no propellers but was driven by a steam engine which worked a powerful pump, drawing in water through the bottom of the boat and discharging it at the sides – it could take in a ton of water in a second and drive the boat at nine knots. At that time propellers were thought to be vulnerable and the emphasis was on safety rather than efficiency, but nowadays all lifeboats are driven by twin screws in tunnels which are both safe and efficient.

The whole coastline north of Islay is served by four lifeboats operating from Islay, Mallaig, the island of Barra at the southern and Stornoway at the northern end of the Outer Hebrides. In my opinion there are still too few lifeboats in the north-west of Scotland.

* * *

Chapter One

The front door of the hotel had been left unlocked for me so I went straight up to our room. Switching on the light I found the carpet rolled back to the middle of the floor and the boards covered with sodden newspapers. My first thought was that I was in the wrong room, but the sight of my wife peacefully asleep reassured me. There was no sign of a leak in the ceiling and all the window panes were whole, so I could not understand where all the water had come from; I learned later that the wind was strong enough to drive the rain under the windows on that side of the hotel. Quietly picking up my bag, I tiptoed to the bathroom. A hot bath is a wonderful institution. I filled it up as far as I dared and just lay in the lap of luxury, thawing out, turning on the hot tap now and again until I was almost cooked. My wet clothes I left in the bath, having rinsed them out in fresh water to get rid of the salt. Dressing myself, I returned to our bedroom where even switching on the light for the second time did not waken Jeanne.

She finally awoke to find me sitting on the roll of carpet, a bottle of whisky in one hand and a glass in the other. Neither of us spoke for a full minute while Jeanne looked at me as if she thought I was a ghost. As I drained my glass her expression changed to relief. She told me that the hotel's wireless had the trawler wave band and she was therefore able to listen to the first part of our conversation with Oban radio. Jack describing the kind of the night must have cheered her up no end; then she heard only: 'Oban radio calling Mallaig lifeboat . . . calling Mallaig lifeboat . . . can you hear me? Over . . .' but no reply from the Mallaig lifeboat, for we were then in the Narrows. She said that she had been terribly afraid when she saw the lifeboat meet the sea at the harbour mouth, for no reply from us convinced her that we were all drowned. Having accepted this she was able, so she said, to sleep peacefully for the remainder of the night! This characteristic acceptance of fate has amazed me more than once since then; when one thinks of it, to worry or lose sleep over probabilities which we have no power to alter is rather silly.

We were provided with a Highland breakfast such as one

seldom sees elsewhere and I allowed none of it to go begging, for my night out had sharpened my appetite. Mrs MacLellan kindly dried out my clothes sufficiently for me to pack them, and we caught the midday train to Morar.

We were met at Morar station by Duncan, the best friend I ever had. He was then in his eightieth year, but looked the picture of health. His almost cherubic face wore its usual happy expression. Nothing was ever too much bother for him, nor have I ever heard of anyone who did not instantaneously like him. He always wore blue reefer jackets and a peaked cap which gave him a nautical air for all the world like a retired ship's captain. Many happy hours have I spent at his fireside, gleaning all sorts of information from his lifetime's experiences. He was a Gaelic scholar of no mean standard and had a library that would have done credit to many a stately home, with many of his books proclaiming on the flyleaf: 'To Duncan, from the author.'

It did not take us long to reach the loch where Duncan's boat was waiting at the small wooden pier. We were quickly under way, heading out towards the lovely wooded islands between which we must pass. It was a beautifully calm day, so calm that with the mirroring effect you were hard put to see where the islands left off and the loch began. It is quite shallow for about a mile until one passes out clear of the islands. Beyond the islands the level drops abruptly, until, between Meoble on the south shore and Swordlands on the north, a depth of 1,017 feet has been recorded. When one considers that at this point the mountains rise almost sheer to over 1,200 feet on both sides and that the loch is only thirty feet above sea-level, the immensity of the hole is unique. It is deeper than any part of the North Sea and to find a comparable depth on the west coast you would have to steam over a hundred miles west until you reached a parallel west of St Kilda. According to Sir Archibald Geikie, Loch Morar is the deepest recorded hollow in the European plateau, with the exception of the submarine hollow fringing southern Scandinavia.

Duncan told me that it was from his boat that they had

measured the depth of the loch at various places, and that there was a ridge of comparatively shallow water between the islands of Brinacory and Allimhara.

His boat was his pride and joy. He and Hugh had built her themselves. She was a lively clinker launch of over 30 feet, powered by an eighteen hp paraffin engine, and could do six or seven knots. She had a fine fo'c'sle cabin, an open hold amidships, a small engine room, and an open cockpit aft of this. She was always spick and span, despite the varied cargoes she carried, ranging from livestock to stores, including coal, for as the loch is fresh water Duncan could work up a wonderful lather when scrubbing down. I have never been able to get over the way he used to lean over the side and fill his kettle! To me, used to the sea, this was the height of luxury. Another thing I found wonderful was the lack of tide. He tied his boat tight to the jetty and she would be there in the morning just as he had left her the night before; no need to allow for rise and fall.

On arrival at Meoble pier we found John Macdonald the stalker, who had come to collect his groceries and any mail there might be. A tall, lean, handsome man with a fine head of snow-white hair, he had been a stalker in Meoble all his life, and his father and grandfather before him. We had spent many happy days in the hills together and I owe him a great deal, for he was an excellent master under whom to serve an apprenticeship in the art of deer-stalking. I have heard it called the sport of kings, and it is certainly a sport for richer men than I, but then I do not think that John would have bothered with me had I been one of the 'gentlemen' who came for a few days' stalking. For the most part they caused him acute anguish, few of them seeming to realize the skill he had to exercise in his battle of wits with so wary an animal on its own ground. He had to know the ground and be able to make a very accurate guess as to what the stag might do. It is necessary to live in a deer forest and know the mountains in all their moods and climatic conditions before it is possible, in the first place, to judge in a given set of circumstances where the deer are likely to be. His diplomacy when restraining his 'gentlemen' from spoiling the whole effort by impatience during the actual approach to the stag was the result of innate Highland courtesy, and on many occasions I knew him to be inwardly seething. There is more in deer-stalking than the stalk: the forest has to be properly managed throughout the year; hinds have to be shot in winter; heather has to be burnt in a ten-to-fifteen-year rotation; and foxes have to be kept down because of the toll they take of the deer calves. Stalkers invariably have a pack of terriers which are put into the cairns to bolt the vixens and kill the cubs. Eagles, buzzards and falcons are usually encouraged, to keep down the grouse whose warning chatter has spoilt many a stalk.

John showed me many things that I, not of the hills, would not have seen for myself. For instance, he would watch a hind with his telescope then turn and say to me: 'She has hidden her calf in that clump of bracken.' I would search with my glass, but no calf would I see.

'Neither can I see it, Tex,' he would say, 'but it's there all right.' And off we would go to make sure. While I watched, he would go in among the bracken and bring out the calf, talking to it in that soft, crooning Gaelic voice of his, until it followed him like a pet lamb. The hind meanwhile would have run a short way off and, having turned, would be standing watching us, always above us, stamping her front feet indignantly and barking as they do when alarmed.

'She's not mad at us,' John would say, 'it's the calf she's wild with.' And he would shoo it towards her. The mother would nuzzle it for a moment before making off slowly up the hill. We would pretend to take no further interest by turning our backs and going in the opposite direction. Having picked a spot where we could spy on her with our glasses, we waited until she hid the calf again but, try as we would, we could never get near that calf again. We have often tried this and always with the same result, and I might add that we were only successful in the first place if it was a very young calf. John is convinced that the mother gives it such a wigging for fraternizing with the enemy that the calf ever after avoids all men like the plague.

Having distributed the stores and mail for the other two families, we made our way up to 'Rifern', Duncan's house, where we were to stay. It was a small cottage typical of the area, having three rooms downstairs and three bedrooms upstairs, but, luxury of luxuries, it also had an added bathroom. We were welcomed by Duncan's wife, a most industrious soul, possessed of boundless energy that would have done credit to a woman of half her years. Her house was absolutely spotless, but not the sort of spotlessness that makes one afraid to sit down, for this was a happy, lived-in house.

We were hustled into the kitchen where we found the table set and three steaming bowls of soup already in their places. I can never yet think of 'Rifern' without associating it with good, wholesome food and plenty of it. No matter at what time of the day or night I arrived at Duncan's house, his wife always had a meal prepared for us. Both he and his son, Hugh, had accompanied me up and down Loch Morar at all sorts of odd hours in the periods I spent there during the war. I was sent back once for a year owing to a game leg which made me grade C, but I eventually managed to convince the MO that I was fit again by racing him over the hills from Lochailort and getting down to the Lodge in time to have two pints of beer on the table before he put in an appearance.

My triumph at getting back into action again was short-lived, for just within the year I was back in hospital with my leg smashed up properly this time. They repaired it very well, but it was never again good enough for Commando work. When I could walk I returned to Meoble, remaining there until the German capitulation in Norway; then, as we were no longer needed, the school was closed and I was pensioned off. It is quite a good leg, except that it gets tired sooner than the other one, but if I wear an elastic device to keep the knee-joint in place I can do as much as the next man.

In addition to Duncan and John the only other family living in Meoble at that time was that of John's late brother Sandy. For general purposes and to avoid confusion the two Mistresses MacDonald were called Mistress John and Mistress Sandy; similarly Mistress MacDonnell was called Mistress Duncan. Members of their families were known by their respective house-names when speaking in English. In Gaelic one distinguishes people by going well back into their genealogy, and at that time all the people in Meoble were fluent Gaelic speakers.

Mistress Sandy had a large family, seven girls and two boys. Theresa, the youngest, was a lovable little blonde elf whose first arrival in Meoble in 1941 coincided with my own. From the time she could walk she was always among the soldiers and quickly made friends with all who wore khaki. A precocious child, she soon built up a sizeable vocabulary of largely military origin; it was strange to hear such a tiny tot talking of bombs, ranges and detonators, and things that were 'pukka'.

Later that evening we went to call on Mistress Sandy. She lived in a similar cottage to John and Duncan, just beyond the shooting lodge. Jeanne and I spent some time in the vicinity of the lodge trying to reconstruct the picture as it was during the war. The canteen, dining-hall and all the huts were gone; all that remained of the army was the wash-house and drying shed, which was built of brick. I'll never forget the fug there used to be in that drying shed, with its two coal stoves going full blast and tier upon tier of wet socks, shirts, battledresses, etc., steaming away. There were always plenty of wet things after a day's training in the hills. It was at the lodge that we had met just before the schools closed down.

When we arrived at Mistress Sandy's house the children all came running to meet us, that is, all except Theresa. We were met at the bottom of the path by Mistress Sandy herself, a kindly, motherly soul. No one will ever know how many meals she gave to soldiers during the war, for hers was always open house. Never an evening passed without its crowd of soldiers round her fire. Theresa, it appeared, was in a huff and was not going to have anything more to do with me – I had let her down, everyone knew she was my sweet-heart and now I had gone off and married an English girl – but a box of chocolates and *Rua*, a book about a red deer calf, helped to convince her that Jeanne was not too bad after all.

In spite of the snow I enjoyed several days' good hind shooting with John and sometimes, armed with nothing more lethal than a couple of telescopes, Jeanne and I stalked roedeer, the smallest and most beautiful of our native deer. They are always to be found in among birch scrub by the lochside where the feeding is better. Stalking them is not particularly easy, for their sight and hearing are much more highly developed than those of the red deer, although their powers of scent are vastly inferior. It has always been a source of amusement to me to see them glance back at the top of an extra big leap as they bound away and, seeing they are being followed, stop and stare as if inviting me to chase them. No one shot roedeer in Meoble; John's stock answer, when taxed with this was: 'Ach, man, they're too nice!'

Most evenings we spent sitting by Duncan's kitchen fire coaxing him to tell us tales of the old days, of the time when the big steamboats used to come to Tarbet, Loch Nevis, to buy herring, and there was a thriving herring industry centred there. When Duncan was a boy there were quite a few houses, a Roman Catholic chapel and a small inn at Tarbet Bay. All that remain today are the chapel and the inn, but it is no longer an inn, for it is occupied by a crofter who manages somehow to scrape a living from the few sheep he runs on the hill. Duncan loved to tell of the time when the proprietor of the inn, never having stocked anything but barrels of whisky before, sent for some barrels of beer to please the crews of the big English steamboats. The beer had to be carted in by road from Fort William to Mallaig and there put aboard Duncan's father's boat. At Tarbet the barrels were offloaded and rolled laboriously up the beach to the inn. It was customary to give a fairly large dram, by way of sampling the new whisky, to the men who brought it. This the proprietor did with the beer, broaching a barrel as soon as it was on the gantry; you can well imagine the unexpected shower bath they had before they got it tapped. The Highland fishermen, tasting this new beverage for the first time, were all agreed that it could not possibly be beer – surely they did not drink this, even in England? Rather than spoil the good name of his inn, the proprietor declared it to be bad and had the whole consignment opened and allowed to run into the sea; he was sure that, whether it was beer or not, the barrels were likely to explode at any moment and might even blow the place up.

It must have been a very prosperous inn all the same, for Duncan, being one of the few local men of trust who could count beyond a certain figure, was always called in once a year at the end of the fishing season to 'do the books'. As the money was kept in herring barrels this must have been quite a business, sovereigns, silver and copper each in their own containers. A fishing boat's sail, usually a new white one, was spread on the floor and the sovereigns were emptied on to it and counted carefully back into the barrel. When all the sovereigns were counted, the barrel was lidded up and the total it contained was painted on the lid; the silver and copper were treated likewise. Then the bills gathered and the accounts reckoned. I have no idea what the price of whisky was seventy years ago, but Duncan never referred to bottles of whisky when telling me tales of his youth; it was always two gallon jars. Those were the days.

By comparison with modern times I suppose life was tough then and I scarcely think fishermen of today would put up with the hardships the men of those days took as a matter of course. Duncan could well remember his father remarking on one occasion, soon after he had started herring fishing, that he would soon make his fortune as he had just sold a few cran of herring at the fabulous price of three shillings and sixpence a cran. A cran of herring is four baskets, that is twenty-eight stone, and the average price today in Mallaig is £5 a cran.

*   *   *

18

Chapter One

All too soon we were away down the Loch and across to the 'Garden of Skye', that is the Sleat peninsula. Here we thought we would find a house to buy, feeling then, though we now know better, that with the drift south from the Highlands we were sure to find a vacant crofter's cottage suitably situated for a fisherman, which was all we really wanted. Until we found a suitable cottage it looked as if Jeanne would have to remain in London; never fond of town life, Jeanne wished to give up her house there as soon as possible. Her mother who saw me, or should I say eyed me from afar, had been far from enthusiastic about her daughter becoming a fisherman's wife; intending her for something more ambitious, she had sent her to Cheltenham Ladies' College as a good start in this direction. After her mother's death, nine months in sole charge of their guest house convinced Jeanne that, however well established the business might be, the ever-increasing regulations, restrictions and red-tape would shortly make it a nightmare to run.

We did not find a croft house on Skye, although there was no shortage of empty ones. Their owners had taken an active part in the drift south, but all of them intended to retire to their old homes; in the meantime the houses could be let furnished to summer visitors and the land attached let to neighbours. This in my opinion is one of the reasons for the depopulation of the Highlands, for so long as a crofter paid his rent, which was usually the figure he got for one week from the summer visitors, he could not be dispossessed. Young people wishing to become crofters had no chance. It is good to know that with the passing of the 1955 Act something is being done by the new Crofters' Commission to rectify this ridiculous state of affairs.

When we had exhausted all our immediate possibilities we returned to the mainland, Jeanne to go back alone to London and I to put my nose to the grindstone.

Of all the varied forms of fishing which I followed in the course of a year, the then comparatively new industry of fishing for basking sharks appealed to me most of all. Hitherto neither I

nor anybody else had made very much money at it, but the industry was then in its infancy, and anyway it was the sport that
appealed to me in the first place.

Basking sharks are the second largest fish in the world, attaining
a length of thirty feet; only the whale-shark of the Pacific is larger.
These sharks appear in the Minch area early in April and remain
until July or August, disappearing as suddenly as they come. They
are plankton feeders, and as they have to be harpooned when
feeding on the surface the mode of fishing is somewhat similar to
whaling, but on a smaller scale. Their value lies in their huge but-
ter-coloured liver, fifteen hundredweights or more, which is best
described as a honeycomb of oil with an extraction rate of eighty
per cent.

In previous years I had been employed as harpoonier with
Gavin Maxwell's sharkfishing venture, but now I wanted to set up
on my own and put into practice the lessons I felt I had learned
from this experience.

Gavin Maxwell and I had first met in Meoble during the war,
he was then a Major of the Scots Guards and Commandant of
another school in the area. After our release from the Special
Forces he had started his sharkfishing venture, with me as his first
employee. Together we had harpooned a great number of sharks,
first of all with hand-harpoons, after the fashion of Moby Dick,
from a thirty-foot launch. In retrospect some of our early hand-
harpoons appear ridiculously inadequate; we might as well have
tried to catch a shark with a kitchen fork. We improved our technique by experience and a great deal of trial and error, until we
arrived at what we considered to be the perfect gun and harpoons,
but not the perfect boat, for we were fishing from a seventy-five
foot, ex-Admiralty, Harbour Defence Motor Launch, powered by
a pair of 160 hp diesels.

I had no boat suitable for this type of fishing but that could be
easily acquired; the difficulty was to get a harpoon gun of sufficient weight, but not heavy enough to shatter the boat when the
harpoon was fired. I asked Jeanne to help me in my search for an

old-fashioned whaling gun, in fact one of the very first guns to be used on whales by the Greenland whalemen in 1732. At that time a gun firing a harpoon was looked upon with scorn by the old-time harpooniers. Its only advantage was that it could hurl a harpoon farther than a man, but this was offset by the noise it made, which scared off the remainder of the whales in the school. As these guns were mounted in the bows of the old-time oar-propelled whaleboats they quickly fell from favour. However, in 1772 they were reintroduced and a good number made. Their use was fostered by the British Arts Council, which offered a bounty of ten guineas to the most successful gunner and a premium of three guineas for each successful shot. Although a number of the whalemen from Peterhead acquired guns, they did not catch on, the harpooniers still preferring the old hand harpoon to any harpoon gun. It was not until 1865, when Svend Foyn, a Norwegian whale-master from Tonsberg, revolutionized the whaling industry by the invention of his shot harpoon, that harpoon guns were accepted by whalemen. Svend Foyn's gun, which was huge by comparison with hand harpoons, was mounted in the bows of a small schooner-rigged steamboat. It fired a harpoon weighing about a hundredweight, with an explosive charge in its nose, whereas the old-time Greener gun fired only a light harpoon of similar weight and design to a hand harpoon. It was one of the original Greener guns that I wanted, or one of similar size. The larger later types of gun would be too big, and explosive-headed harpoons worse than useless for sharkfishing, as the liver would be ruined by the explosion. The only two that I knew of belonged to the Island of Soay Shark Fisheries Limited and, as far as I know, I had been the first man to use this type of gun on a shark when the infant company, under Gavin Maxwell, came into being. I tried to obtain a gun from the company, but they were not prepared to part with one.

My dutiful wife made a list of all the London gunmakers and worked her way stoically through them, mostly on foot. She considered personal contact more likely to produce results and enjoyed watching the varied expressions on the assistants' faces as she made her odd request. It was an unusual query anyway and certainly unexpected from a girl. Some were courteous, but unable to help; some were frankly incredulous, deciding that the lady was definitely unhinged. One recommended the British Museum, others passed her gaily round the same circle, and yet another sent her to the fishing-tackle shop in the Mall where they offered her a toy for shooting fish in frogman-style. Mr Greener's elephant trophy in his London showroom floored her almost literally. The manager rushed to her aid but could not help her in her quest, although he offered to make us a gun, the most helpful suggestion she received. She even tried a film studio property-room with the same result. I have heard it said that you can get anything you want in London, but it failed to produce a one-and-half-inch-bore harpoon gun. In all fairness we did not give Messrs Harrods a chance to make good their claim that they can supply anything, but that was because we did not know about it until much later.

After much wasted effort on the part of both Jeanne and me, a gun was finally located by Mr Leyton Greener of W. W. Greener, Gunmakers, Birmingham. His firm had not only made all the equipment I had used when fishing with Maxwell, but had produced some of the first whaling guns, to which I have already referred. I immediately went to Birmingham and saw Mr Greener, who knew exactly what I wanted, for he had spent some weeks at sea with us when Maxwell was experimenting with different types of gun. This was exactly the sort of gun I had been hoping to find and I considered myself lucky, for I do not believe there are half a dozen of them in the country.

Mr Greener was not over-enthusiastic about it, for he felt that the loading system should be modified. Afraid that it would not be ready to try out during the coming season, I persuaded him, much against his will, to let me take it as it was. He had already had the barrel tested and found it to be in perfect condition despite its age.

This type of gun is muzzle-loading, you simply pour the measured gunpowder down the barrel and ram an inch-thick circular felt wad behind it. At the breach end there were two nipples similar to those on a Primus stove but with larger apertures. Over these were placed two tophat-shaped percussion caps which were fired off simultaneously by one hammer, thus igniting the main charge. There was a flashplate, in actual fact a rounded brass cover for the hammer – which was intended to prevent the gunner from singeing his beard should any of the explosion blow backwards through the nipples. The gun was one-and-half-inch bore and weighed almost a hundredweight, the barrel being three feet long and almost an inch thick. I asked him to make a number of harpoons with hand-forged nickel-chrome steel barbs, similar to the ones I ultimately used with the Soay Company. My business finished, I spent an interesting afternoon in Mr Greener's factory before catching the train for London.

Some time later I exchanged several letters with Harry Thompson, who had joined the Soay Company the year I left. I told him that I had acquired a harpoon gun and intended to start sharkfishing independently. Very soon afterwards he rang me up from Glasgow suggesting that, as I had no suitable boat of my own, I might like to go into partnership with a friend of his, George Langford, an ex-Army Captain then living in the island of Raasay. Apparently a tentative arrangement that Harry had made with Langford, that the Company should hire his boat had fallen through. He had very little fishing experience of any kind and knew nothing of sharkfishing but, having listened to Harry's yarns of sharking, he was terribly disappointed that he was not to take an active part. I rang him up from London and found him to be more than willing to come in with me on any sharkfishing project. He also told me that there were a number of crofthouses on Raasay and one large house built by a retired minister which were vacant, and he strongly recommended that we should come up and see them. This seemed worth investigating, so once again Jeanne and I set out together for the Highlands.

To get to Raasay one catches the daily steamer from Mallaig to

Portree in the isle of Skye. On her way she calls at Raasay with mail and passengers. We were met by Langford, a lightly built man in his late thirties. He took us up to his home, a large old-fashioned house which had been the residence of the Estate Factor in the days of the MacLeods of Raasay. It was not in very good condition, but then nothing in Raasay seemed to be in a good state of repair, not even Langford's boat, although she was sound enough.

We met the same sort of situation here that we had in Sleat for, although there appeared to be plenty of vacant crofthouses, none of them were for sale. An interview with the late minister's brother proved equally fruitless. Three of his next of kin shared equally in the bequest of the house and its contents, which included a number of rare Gaelic books, and none could agree as to its future – a situation which was further complicated by the fact that one of them lived in America.

It was arranged before we left the island that I should go shark-fishing with Langford, provided that we could get a market for the raw liver. There were quite a number of firms interested in the oil but I found it very hard to interest anyone in the raw liver. I was about to give it up when I succeeded in persuading the late Mr Gordon Davidson of the Scottish Fish Meal Manufacturing Company to try it out. As one of the directors of the Soay Company he was well acquainted with shark-liver and its potentialities. He was to pay us according to the percentage of oil he got from the livers but he could not so far forecast the coming season's price per ton of whale oil, which would govern the market. We started the season not knowing whether our venture was to pay or not . . . it didn't.

First of all the gun did not behave properly. Every time I fired it sheets of flame blew back through the nipples and under the flashplate, burning my face. In desperation I used three blankets cut up in strips and wrapped round the flashplate in a vain attempt to keep it from burning me. The harpoons ordered locally were not of the metal or design I wanted, and unfortunately the Greener harpoons were not ready. Worst of all, on the few occasions when we did arrive in Mallaig with a cargo of liver, it was almost impossible to get away to sea again: the local rum possessed a stronger attraction than the sharks.

Basically the gun was good enough and, had I not been so impatient, but taken Mr Greener's advice and had the firing mechanism modified, I am sure it would have been perfect. We did catch a fair number of sharks despite our many setbacks, but I had very little chance to test my pet theories. I cannot say I was sorry when in the middle of the season I screwed off my gun and, taking all my gear ashore, prepared to clear off to London.

I was actually in Mallaig station making for the train when someone told me that the Soay Company also was in trouble. Harry Thompson had got into difficulties which had resulted in his catcher running ashore, where she was likely to become a total loss. My informant had also heard that the Soay Company was giving up.

After a great deal of trouble exchanging telegrams I managed to get Harry on the other end of a telephone line. He confirmed that the Company was going into liquidation and that a sale of assets was to be held in Mallaig when he returned with whatever he could salvage of his catcher. He also added that the manager was coming up to meet him and supervise this.

The sale was to be by public auction, but I felt it was unlikely that there would be much opposition, for thus far no one had made anything of sharkfishing, and a few had lost heavily. I remained convinced that, as long as there was a market for the oil, sharkfishing, if worked properly, could be made an economic success. This was a heaven-sent opportunity to buy the first gun I had caught a shark with, and some harpoons that I knew and could trust – in fact everything that a shark fisherman could want. I inquired of Harry the whereabouts of 'Sugan', the old muzzle loader I had used with Maxwell. He told me that it was at the factory in Soay. I dearly wanted that gun, for I knew every one of her moods and idiosyncrasies and had been the first man to use her on a shark, although the old girl was nearly a hundred years old. She was really a whaling gun of the type for which we had been searching, but to make it safer and more reliable Mr Greener had had the nipples and percussion caps replaced by a Martini action which fired a .38 blank to ignite the main charge, which was twelve drams of Peter Hawker coarse gun-powder.

Harry had been using that season, I think for the first time, a small breech-loading Kongsberg (Norway) gun, which he found to be good enough although it had several faults, chief among which was the small bore of the barrel. Because of this he had to use steel harpoon shafts and they were always bending, which rendered them useless; furthermore these did not conform to B.S.S. and were therefore difficult to obtain.

It was not long before the manager, Harry and I, foregathered aboard the crippled *Nancy Glen* to do our bargaining. Whether the rest was actually sold by auction or not I do not know, but I gathered that I was the only man interested in the fishing gear. Before I left the *Nancy Glen*'s fo'c'sle I had bought two guns, my old friend 'Sugan' and her sister gun, the latter being the one Maxwell had used himself, and as many harpoons and shafts as I could lay my hands on.

Chapter Two

The worrying question of where we were to find a house near the Minch fishing grounds with the necessary anchorage for a boat was becoming ever more pressing. Jeanne had found a buyer for her house and was due to move in early August, and to crown this there were to be three of us in October. It was reading an article on salmon fishing in some periodical that gave me the brain-wave. Leaving Jeanne sitting reading in the garden I went into the house, without mentioning my intention in case nothing should come of it, and, lifting the telephone, got in touch with Mr Powrie in Perth.

'Tex Geddes here. What do you intend to do with your cottage on Soay now that your lease of the salmon fishing has expired?' I asked.

He replied: 'Sell it. Do you want it?'

It was as easy as that. I slipped quietly back to my chair, making no mention of my triumph. My wife was maddeningly uninterested in my brief absence, or perhaps refrained from comment in the belief that it was due to natural causes. Unable to restrain myself any longer I burst out with: 'How would you like to live on Soay?'

Jeanne did not reply at once, but gave me that long knowing look, which I have since come to know so well.

'Come on, out with it! What scheme have you in mind now?' she said.

'I have no scheme,' I replied, 'but I have found a house with all the necessary qualifications.' And I told her of my conversation with Mr Powrie.

The house was, in fact, a small corrugated-iron bungalow, lined throughout with varnished wood which gave the interior a pleasantly Scandinavian appearance which belied its rather unpromising exterior. There were only two bedrooms, a living-room and a small kitchen, but this would be adequate for our immediate needs. The large windows gave an all-round view and made the house light and cheerful.

We both knew Soay, for I had taken Jeanne there on a holiday the previous summer, and I had practically lived on the island when fishing with Maxwell. We knew the house to be in fairly good order for we had visited the salmon fishermen who had occupied it while we were there. Mr Powrie suggested that we should meet on Soay and there complete the deal. He intended to visit the island towards the end of the salmon-fishing season to supervise the removal of his fishing gear.

The prospect of this house was a load off our minds and I particularly was more than pleased because Soay was, I thought, the ideal place for me; not only did it have an excellent harbour but it was right in the middle of the sharking grounds.

The island of Soay lies to the south of Skye, just below the Cuillins, which so completely dominate it that when approaching from the Point of Sleat one gets the impression that it is part of the Cuillin mass. It is almost two islands, the narrow harbour on the north almost meeting Camas nan Gall, the village bay, on the south. Its total area amounts to little more than 3,000 acres. It is not very fertile and there is a good deal of birch and rowan scrub. Three miles long and two miles wide, Soay was for generations part of the estates of the MacLeod of Dunvegan, and was at this time owned by the Island of Soay Shark Fisheries Limited, under the directorship of the Duke of Hamilton. Its past history is obscured by a fog of controversy so dense that all efforts to penetrate it were brought up short by the fire which had destroyed certain of the MacLeod records. It is the common belief that the island was uninhabited before the last of the Highland Clearances; therefore it is interesting to note that the island was inhabited at least in 1695, for Martin Martin in his *Description of the Western Islands of Scotland* observes: 'There has been no venomous creature ever seen in this little isle until within these two years last that a black and white big serpent was seen by one of the inhabitants, who killed it; they believe it came from the opposite coast of Skye ...' He also notes: 'It is full of bogs and fitter for pasture than for cultivation.'

Nevertheless, it is a beautiful little island. The path from the village to the harbour is lined with silver birch and at the harbour itself the air is heavy with the scent of honeysuckle all through the summer. Spring comes early to Soay, bringing snowdrops, daffodils, primroses and bluebells in profusion. The bluebells particularly are everywhere, among the bracken at the side of the path, in the woods, and carpeting the little haymeadows. The peaty soil is ideal for rhododendrons and azaleas; some lovely specimens of the latter were imported by Gavin Maxwell. There are thirteen lochans, some with marshy reed-fringed margins, some scooped out of the bare rock, and yet others which spread a quilt of wax-white water-lilies in their season. Of the ten families then living on the island, the greater majority of the men were lobster-fishermen. There was a school and a post office with an antiquated radio telephone link to the village of Elgol, three miles away, the nearest inhabited point on Skye. The telephone was used only by the postmistress for the transmission of telegrams. As there was no shop on the island, everyone had their supplies sent out from Mallaig, either by MacBrayne's steamer on Saturdays, or the forty-foot ML *Islander* on Wednesdays.

We arranged to stay with Sandy Campbell, a crofter on Soay, until we met Mr Powrie and completed the deal. Sandy had let us a bedroom and a sitting-room. Mistress Campbell was in the unique position of being the island's official schoolteacher with her own twin daughters as her only pupils; the remainder of the island's children were either below school age or already at secondary schools in Skye. She was a tall, handsome woman to whom many of the islanders were wont to turn for advice. Sandy had by then retired after an active life as a merchant seaman. After leaving the Merchant Service he had for some years been running a weekly mail and freight service from Soay to Mallaig with his fishing boat *Marys*, until she was lost in the latter part of 1947. The boat caught fire soon after leaving Mallaig and he and his passengers were lucky to escape with their lives. I was in Mallaig that night and saw them off. I don't remember why I waited on the pier but I do remember being horror-struck when I saw the flames some miles out. There was no way of knowing how long the fire had been going, nor was I then certain that it was Sandy's *Marys*. I raced for the *Gannet* and got her engine running (this was Maxwell's thirty-foot launch we used sharkfishing). While casting off a shout of: 'Is that you, Tex?' told me that I was not alone in my anxiety, and seconds later the village constable leaped unceremoniously off the end of the quay down on to the *Gannet*'s deck. Fortunately he was familiar with boats and took the helm while I rummaged in the fo'c'sle with the aid of his torch for the paraffin lamp which served as sailing lights. I found it, lit it, and ran it up the mast, for the night was as black as pitch, and we felt that, if Sandy could see a light making towards him, he would know that they had been seen. We thought that we might be able to tow the burning boat into shallow water, but when we reached her she was too far gone. I shall never forget the explosion caused by a barrel of paraffin bursting in the hold and the tracer-like effect of a box of shotgun cartridges, which I later learned were in the mailbag. She was a strong little boat and it hurt me to see her go like that. Sandy and some Soay men were in his small dinghy when we got out to her. There were six of them, packed like sardines in a tin, and one of them baling with a wellington boot. They were lucky the night was comparatively calm, for they would not have gone very far in such an overloaded boat. It was heartrending to see Sandy bare his head as she went down. She was not insured so he was unable to replace her.

There was amongst them an old man on his first trip to Mallaig for fourteen years. He told me that he was certain that I would come out to them, but he couldn't see my light for the flames had blinded him and he could still see nothing. He always wore a pair of very strong glasses and it was not until we were all aboard the *Sea Leopard*, Maxwell's HDML, that I noticed that they were black with smoke. I removed and cleaned them before setting them back on his nose. With all the excitement it had never occurred to the old man that his 'blindness' could be so easily cured and that I was not the wizard he took me for in his first moments of regained sight.

Sandy's was the finest house on the island, having been completely rebuilt in 1939. It was the only house that could boast the luxury of a bathroom, which was added as a lean-to, and like the rest of the house was built of stone. His wife took a great pride in the little walled garden in front of it, where there were some lovely old-fashioned roses, veronica and rhododendron bushes, one wall of which was a bank of honeysuckle. His croft was equally well kept, for the little haymeadow at the back of the house was the greenest patch in the island, providing ample hay for his two cows. He was a happy man, well-known for his kindness; very few people visited Soay without tasting his hospitality.

We arrived in Mallaig at midday on August the 16th, 1949, timing our arrival to coincide with the departure of MacBrayne's weekly excursion steamer which runs to Loch Coruisk during the tourist season. Loch Coruisk lies in a great rocky amphitheatre at the foot of the Cuillins, just beyond Loch Scavaig. Above it towers the main ridge, dominated by jagged peaks, giving the impression of the shattered edge of a giant cauldron. Each year hundreds of tourists visit the loch, for it is said to be the grandest (I think it's the gloomiest) view in Scotland. When the steamer dropped anchor we could see Ronald Macdonald in his launch *Hetty* which was to take us to the island, after the steamer had disgorged all her passengers. By then the sun had broken through, making it a very pleasant sail across the Sound of Soay to the bay. We landed on the beach just below Sandy's house, and there we found both Sandy and Harry MacDonald, Mr Powrie's foreman. Harry had been instructed to let us have the key of the bungalow when we arrived on the island. As quickly as decency would allow we swallowed our tea, for although we had visited it the previous summer we had not paid a great deal of attention to the layout of the bungalow, and we now spent an hour or two mentally arranging the furniture.

We had a protracted correspondence with Mr Powrie at his salmon-fishing station in Ardnamurchan. He promised to come to see us but was unable to do so for some time. When he eventually arrived at the end of September, Jeanne had gone to Inverness, where our son was born on October 2nd.

Although Mr Powrie was prepared to sell the bungalow, he wished to retain his tenancy of the croftland on which it stood. I was perfectly content that he should do so but, as I soon learned, it was a condition that created complications under Crofting Law. In an effort to overcome these difficulties, I made various suggestions which I hoped might meet the requirements of the law but, as it turned out, the lawyers refused to entertain it. The ultimate result was that I received a letter from Mr Powrie in which he said that, on the advice of his legal advisers, he had decided to withdraw the property from sale. I tried every argument I could think of in order to make him change his mind but he was adamant. Eventually I had to admit defeat.

I did not return immediately to Soay but went to Inverness, anxious to see my son and heir, but hating to bring such depressing news, which, however, Jeanne took surprisingly well.

I had no experience of babies, never having had any desire to handle them. If I thought of them at all, it was as leaky little things that no power under heaven could stop once they started howling. This one seemed strangely quiet as we pushed the pram round the hospital grounds, so much so that we often stopped to have a look at it, just to make sure it was still alive. Jeanne remained ten days in Raigmore hospital after the baby was born in order to arrive in Mallaig the night before the weekly Soay steamer. We had to spend that night in Mallaig as the steamer left at seven in the morning. Whether by coincidence or design we found ourselves in the same hotel room as that which we had occupied on the night of the lifeboat episode. It is not always easy to cope successfully with a small baby in a hotel, but Mrs MacLellan provided all the facilities that she would have for her own grandchildren.

We were astir early but as it was blowing a gale I was not any too sure whether the steamer would be able to call at Soay and, if she did, whether Neil, the ferryman, would be able to take us ashore. Leaving Jeanne at the hotel, I went down to the pier to find out what the captain thought about it. This was the same steamer – now under the command of Captain MacLeod, aboard which the lifeboat's crew had thawed out that night in Kyle of Lochalsh. He assured me: 'Aye, we'll put you ashore somewhere on Soay. We'll wire Neil from Canna to meet us at the north harbour if there is too much weather in the bay.'

Hurrying back to the hotel, I collected my wife and child and soon we were being heaved and tossed about as we butted our way towards Eigg. To get to Soay in the comfort of the steamer we had to do a tour of the Small Isles, calling first at Eigg, Rum and Canna and finally at Soay. After this the steamer returned to Mallaig with the freight and mail she had collected.

There were a number of passengers aboard that morning, amongst whom we found the current Soay missionary. We were not long out of Mallaig when Jeanne decided to go below and have her breakfast, leaving me to take care of the baby. No sooner had she gone than it began creating hell. I lifted it out of the cot and ascertained that it was quite dry and that no pins were sticking into it. There was nothing else I could do, for if it was hungry I could not help it, and diagnosed seasickness, but so far without the sick. To my relief Jeanne soon returned in great spirits, saying; 'I've had a huge breakfast. It seems that everyone except Commander MacEwen and ourselves is seasick.' She quickly and miraculously quietened the baby and I went below to see what they had left for me. Commander MacEwen, indifferent to the storm and calmly reading his newspaper, was still the only other passenger in the dining-saloon. He owns the small but fertile island of Muck, which lies about four miles sou'west of Eigg. I made an excellent breakfast before hurrying back to my wife.

Soon after this I noticed that the motion of the boat had changed and she was now rolling violently instead of punching into it; we were forced to close the windows because the spray was now being driven against the saloon on deck where we had installed ourselves. We were to discover that it was too rough to call at Eigg and, even if the ferry boat had been able to come out, there was such a sea running that she might have been smashed up alongside the steamer.

The steamer did not call at Rum, either, but was able to call at Canna, this being the only island in the group that can boast a pier big enough for a steamer to get alongside. There we had quite a wait transferring mails and cargo, so Jeanne and I came out on deck, where we met Commander MacEwen once again. He would have to go back to Mallaig and try his luck next mailboat day. Before we left Canna the wind altered to nor'west, which would enable us to get ashore at the village bay on Soay. As there is no steamer pier on Soay, everything and everyone going to the island had to be ferried ashore in stages: from steamer to small open motor launch; and from there into a dinghy to be rowed ashore. We had to jump down into the little motor launch from a steel door in the ship's side – all very well on a calm day, but quite an adventure on a rough one. I have not heard of anyone getting a ducking but mailbags flung with characteristic gay abandon sometimes missed the boat all too literally. I find it difficult to decide whether this lack of a pier is not a blessing in disguise, as it probably accounts for the absence of both rats and mice. The only wild animals on the island are otters, hedgehogs, rabbits and pygmy shrews.

Man has been waging war on rats for countless generations and mostly he has broken even, sometimes he has been triumphant, but I think one of the worst defeats on record must have been on the island of North Rona where, around 1760, the last of the inhabitants was found dead of starvation. An influx of rats, perhaps originating with a pregnant female arriving in a bag of meal, literally ate the islanders out of house and home, for they, being unfamiliar with the brutes, seem to have had no idea how to deal with them. The rats had no natural source of food as they have on other islands where they can pick a living between the tide marks, for the coast of North Rona is rocky and the swell such that this hunting-ground is denied them. It may be that this grisly tale accounts for the almost superstitious horror of rats that some of the Soay people had. While with today's improved communications such an invasion of Soay might not be disastrous, it would be a serious economic blow when not even simple precautions are taken to outwit them.

The remainder of that year was spent either househunting or searching for a suitable boat to have another go at the sharks, and although I did not find a house I managed to acquire a boat. Langford, with his boat once again on the beach, was only too glad to find a buyer for her. I found him meticulously fair when reporting on the boat's condition and he had her dried by the time I arrived at Raasay, so that I could examine her thoroughly. She was in a very bedraggled state and sadly in need of paint. The engine, a twenty-six hp petrol-paraffin Kelvin, looked to be in a deplorable condition, but this dilapidation was largely superficial. She was a good, sound boat but nothing seemed to work properly. The sail had started life as a drifter's mizzen, but someone in Raasay had cut a bit off to make it a more suitable size, if a most peculiar shape. It defied description, for I tried it upside down many times and it worked just as well that way. She was called the *Traveller* and was built in Macduff on the east coast, a Fifie of thirty-four feet overall, twelve-foot beam drawing four feet eight. Built of larch on natural bend oak frames, she was an exceedingly strong little craft. She had a small fo'c'sle with a coal cooking stove, and a large hold, as the engine was placed as far aft as it could be. There was a winch on deck just aft of amidships, and a small wheelhouse with the engine controls to hand, so I would be quite capable of taking her home myself as long as the engine kept going.

After a trial run, George pocketed my cheque and wished me a Merry Christmas and I turned her nose for Kyle of Lochalsh. It must have been an uneventful trip for I can remember no part of it, but I do remember my stay in Kyle. As there were no lights of any kind in the boat, I had no intention of sailing at night; I was not particularly worried about being run down, but rather was afraid that the engine might fail and I might be unable to get it going in the dark. On arrival at Kyle I found a berth alongside a 'puffer',[1] which to my joy was loaded with coal so I soon got a fire going as the fo'c'sle was very damp. I had neither mattress nor blankets, only the sail, which I arranged on one of the bunks in such a way that I had a mattress of sorts below and a cover over me. This with the aid of my duffel coat and a pair of sheepskin gauntlets was my bed, so I kept the stove well stoked during the night. Next morning the weather was so bad that neither the puffer nor I ventured out. When Sunday dawned calm and frosty, I was wakened early by one of the puffer's crew shouting down the hatch: 'We're awa', Jock!'

Being fully dressed, I tumbled on deck, started my engine and left Kyle with them, eating my breakfast on my way down to Mallaig. It was not a very interesting breakfast, a cold tin of peas eaten with a teaspoon – all I had been able to persuade a Kyle grocer to part with without a ration book.

I found Mallaig harbour full of herring boats tied up for the weekend, but managed to find a berth alongside the *Concord*, a Buckie ringnetter. By this time the inadequacy of my breakfast was making itself felt and, knowing her crew, I was soon installed in her warm fo'c'sle eating a first-class feed of delicious thick, brown stew. After this we sat yarning round the fo'c'sle table and drinking mugs of tea until someone turned on the wireless for the shipping forecast: 'Attention all shipping. Severe gales south to sou'west imminent in sea area Hebrides.'

Having no desire to be storm-stayed any longer, I thanked my

1 Small steam coaster.

hosts and made off up the pier in search of some paraffin, for there was not enough in the tanks for safety. Before I left Mallaig I rigged the sail ready to haul up, for if the meteorological office was right I would get plenty of wind, although there was none so far.

The first part of my journey was monotonously calm, but as I got up abreast of the Point of Sleat the wind began to grow, so I raised the sail. On rounding Sleat the wind grew and grew and in a very short time was blowing a full gale. The engine gave me no trouble whatsoever, but ran beautifully the whole way, requiring only a periodical oiling, but I cannot say the same for the sail, for, on trying to lower it when the strength of wind was such that I thought it would carry it away, the block jammed and I had to cut it down. Luckily it was almost high water so I got into the north harbour. There is a stony bar across the mouth, and it can only be entered when there is a sufficient depth of water over this. Some years ago I painted huge white numbers on the rock on the starboard side when entering to indicate the depth of water over the bar. Eight of the Soay motor boats were anchored here in winter, the remainder being hauled up in the village bay.

My worry now was how to get ashore after anchoring the boat for the night, for I had no dinghy. Luckily, however, Donald MacDonald had seen me coming and was even then waiting for me in his dinghy at the head of the harbour.

During the night the wind increased and, although I knew nothing of it until the morning, it was one of the worst gales – and certainly the highest tide – I have experienced since I have known Soay. It must have been fantastically high, for Sandy's dinghy (the one he had taken to when the *Mary*'s went on fire), although hauled up not only to the head of the beach but right across to the other side of the road, was washed away and smashed to pieces at the head of the village bay.

One woman was up all night rescuing her hens; the whole lot, shed and all, blew into the sea. Although I know some of them were drowned, there still seemed to be an amazing collection of assorted poultry in all stages of growth around her house. She had some of the oddest-looking hens I ever saw; I have no idea what breed they were as no one on the island ever called them anything other than 'barenecks'. I am still none the wiser. They had long, thin necks completely devoid of feathers, and the ugly wrinkled skin was as red as a turkey-cock's wattles. Another oddity was characterized by what I can only describe as a 'tourie on its bonnet' instead of a comb. These I later discovered were descendants of Hooded Arrans, which had been distributed by the then Board of Agriculture about fifty years earlier in an effort to improve the local hens.

I was soon busy overhauling the boat. Scraping off all the old paint before repainting her made all the difference to her appearance, and several new parts in the engine a great improvement in her performance. Immediately after the trial run I set off to Eigg to look over an empty cottage, and arrived there just before dark. As it was a calm, frosty night, I left the boat at the pier and made my way up through the fields to the tenant farmer's house on whose land the cottage was supposed to be. He invited me in for tea but quickly dispelled my hopes, explaining that the estate had taken the house back as they wanted to use it as a weekend cottage for fishing. There were others empty on the island and he suggested I should go and see the Factor about them. Rather sadly I left him to go and try my luck with the Factor that night, yet it was my intention to leave for home as soon as possible, for so far it was a lovely moonlit night . . . I wish I had.

I do not remember much about the Factor, only that he was a charming old man on the point of retiring and that he was unable to help as he had orders that none of the empty cottages were to be sold or let, on the pretext that they would be required for estate workers. He was very reluctant to let me go; nothing would have pleased him better than a few hours yarning about sharkfishing, that being the only thing he seemed to be interested in.

It was raining when I left his house and the wind had shifted into the south and was blowing quite hard. Worrying about the boat I hurried down to the pier, for it was full moon and about the time of a high spring tide. She was bumping rather badly, as there is not much shelter at Eigg pier. With a couple of heavy motor tyres between her and the pier by way of fenders I prepared to stay for the night. By this time the fo'c'sle was a more comfortable place than it had been when I bought the boat. I had a comfortable bed with plenty of blankets, pots and pans, plates and knives and things, and the grub locker had a goodly store of tins. There was very little hope of any sleep, for I would have to keep shifting the boat farther up the pier as the tide came in. The pier slopes gradually down towards the sea and at high tide she might mount it if she were not far enough up, and then at the turn of the tide I would have to move her back again or she would ground.

The wind strengthened during the night and several times I had to go on deck to tie ropes, and shift fenders to more advantageous positions. At high tide (the south wind had made it abnormally high) the sea was breaking clean over the rocks to windward of the pier and washing right over it, at times cascading down on my deck. I did not like this, so I started up the engine and went off a short distance, dropped an anchor and paid out the rope as I came back to the pier. Making her bow ropes fast to the pier, I hauled back on the anchor, presenting my stem to the wind a boat's length off the pier. This stopped the water coming aboard, but it was not long before one of her bow ropes broke and I brought up from below about four fathoms of very heavy chain to put in its place. Slackening off the anchor I hauled the boat to the pier with the remaining rope, and making one end fast to her bow I jumped ashore and shackled the other end of the chain to an iron ring embedded in one of the huge stone blocks of which the pier was made. This should hold her, I thought, and the weight of the cabin would quieten her down. While I was watching her behaviour from the shelter of the low wall by the pier a huge sea crashed on the rocks behind me and broke over the pier; I was almost washed away, saving myself by clinging to the wall for dear life. The weight of water which struck the *Traveller* must have been colossal, for she pulled the stone block, complete with its ring, right out of the pier. As it fell it carried several feet of her rail away with it and yanked her ahead to butt the pier stem-on before blowing away out. Luckily, the anchor I had previously dropped held her; everything else appeared to have broken. I did not think she would stick it long there, for I had little faith in the anchor and much less in the rope, and, unlike Parahandy, I did not 'paas and consider', but, soaked to the skin anyway, I pulled off my seaboots, and flung them as far up the pier out of reach of the seas as I could, and dived right in after her. A good enough swimmer, I did not take long to get out to her; grabbing one of the motor tyres, I hauled myself aboard and quickly shifted the anchor rope from her stern to her nose, where she would not put so much strain on it. It seemed an eternity before I got the engine started, but once it was going I felt better; the anchor rope could part if it wanted. By this time the tide was fast ebbing and it was almost daybreak. I soon discovered that the boat was leaking very badly and I began to pump for all I was worth; I do not remember being cold, but I must have pumped her for at least two hours almost non-stop. As the tide ebbed the wind decreased and, when daylight came, I went back to the pier and stopped the engine to save the paraffin. There I met the estate ferryman, Archie MacDonald, and, telling him of my misfortune, I apologized for breaking up his pier, but it was only when he saw the vacant space from which the block had been pulled that he would believe me. He took over the pump from me while I looked for the leak. I found to my horror that the *Traveller* knocked her forefoot right off when she rammed the pier, leaving an ugly splintered space between the stem and the keel. Soon Archie's brother arrived and, handing over the pump to him, Archie hurried off up to his house and returned with a flask of tea and some massive bacon sandwiches. I really wolfed the food – somehow things never look so bad when your belly is full – but I suddenly found myself very tired and so weak that I had to ask Archie to start my engine for me. There was really nothing I could do in Eigg to repair the boat; I would have to get her to Mallaig, and I felt sure that I could still summon up sufficient life to pump her all the way. With the sail set to help my speed, away I went, as fast as she would go, hoping to be able to win the fourteen-mile race with the leaks. The engine, I hoped, once oiled, would need no further attention until I got there. There was not a drop of water in her when I left – Archie had seen to that – nevertheless I started pumping as soon as I was clear of the islands. The pump, an old-fashioned plunger type with a long handle, was worked from the deck. It was well worn but it worked well for me that day. The tiller was lashed so that I could give all my time to the pump and I certainly needed to, for I never managed to get her pumped right out. To relieve the monotony, and also my aching arms, I played a game, counting aloud two hundred strokes before leaving the pump to re-set the tiller and have a look at the amount of water in the bilges. Then I tried humming several tunes to see which of them I could keep the best time to, and found 'The Road to the Isles' quite convenient to fit in, perhaps because I was making all speed for the end of it.

No ancient mariner was ever more glad to make a landfall than I was to reach Mallaig that day. I had to stop pumping at the entrance to Mallaig harbour, lower the sail and unlash the tiller, for I needed complete control over her among the fishing fleet. Rounding the end of the fishquay, I held her straight for the beach and ran her up as far as she would go. I had just made it for, when I went down to stop the engine, the floorboards were afloat; very little more water would have drowned the engine.

The first thing I had to do was wire Jeanne that I was safe in Mallaig but that the *Traveller* had suffered some slight damage. I learned at the post office that Archie had got in touch with them immediately after I had left Eigg, to tell them that I was on my way to Mallaig with a boat as leaky as a basket, pumping all the way. They had looked out for me from the top of the hill, watching my progress until I was almost in the harbour. Although I did not need assistance, I appreciated Archie's thought, which would have set the wheels in motion had I been seen to be in difficulties.

When I failed to arrive home the same night as I had promised, I expected Jeanne to be a little worried, but it was not until my return from Mallaig that I learned just how worried she was before my wire arrived. There was at that time living on Soay a young man in his late twenties who was both deaf and dumb. We were great friends and spent a great deal of time together shooting rabbits. He had no knowledge of the deaf and dumb alphabet but we were able to communicate with each other surprisingly well, distinguishing each person on the island by indicating a physical characteristic or imitating some mannerism such as the hesitation induced by a stutter. For white he would touch his teeth, and for black his rubber boots. Although he could not write, he could draw wonderfully well, and always carried a notebook and pencil. The morning after my departure for Eigg he had stationed himself at the south end of the island to watch for me with his binoculars. He saw the boat leave Eigg with the sail set but soon a shower of rain hid me from view. As I was on my way to Mallaig and not Soay as he expected, when the shower cleared, he could no longer see me. He searched the sea with his binoculars but I was nowhere to be seen, and running back home he drew for his mother a picture of my leaving Eigg with the sail set, adding the rain which blotted out the boat, then another picture of Eigg with no boat. Convinced that I had gone to the bottom, he created a great fuss which luckily the arrival of my telegram put a stop to. This telegram also shattered the hopes of one lonely bachelor who, to a circle of his cronies the night before when my non-appearance was under discussion, had come away with: 'If Texie is trowned, I sink I will try for Cheanne myself. She will be a goot enough wife for me!'

Charlie Henderson, the Mallaig boat-builder, soon put in another forefoot and patched up the rail of the *Traveller*, and in a day or two she was as good as ever.

Chapter Three

I spent a few more days on a series of wild-goose chases before at last I succeeded in acquiring a roof. I learned that Lady Katherine Grant, who owned a holiday house about a mile out of Mallaig, wanted a caretaker to live in the house the year round; she used it for a few weeks of the summer and let it for the remainder. It was agreed that we should take up residence at Glasnacardoch, bringing our own furniture out of store. This arrangement suited both parties, for the furniture would more than fill our rooms and save Lady Katherine from bringing over any extra.

It was not long before we made ourselves comfortable in the rooms which had been redecorated for us, but I did not meet Lady Katherine until Easter. I liked her at once. A very tall, slender woman with dark, curly hair, she was one of those extremely energetic people who give the impression of being incapable of sitting still for long. I was later to discover that she was also a very capable person, and therefore always appreciative of any little job I did for her, for I was not included in the agreement Jeanne had with her, and was free to come and go as I wished. This was later to mean climbing in at the kitchen window in the early hours of the morning when I came home from the sea unexpectedly. Now that we had a home, although not exactly what we would have wished, I could go to sea for another go at sharkfishing, but this time fitted out as I had always wanted to be and completely independent of any shore base.

When fishing with the old Soay Company I had always wanted to try removing the liver from the sharks at sea, but I never got the opportunity and was determined to try it now. The previous year, when fishing with Langford, we had still beached the sharks. The only man among the few in the district who had been with the old Soay Company and was likely to go with me on such a venture was John McInerney; the remainder were either herring-fishing or in the boat-hiring business. His experience of sharkfishing was only part of a season but I felt sure that what he might lack in experience he would certainly make up in enthusiasm and in the most important qualification of all, youth and strength. He had that certain devil-may-careness that somehow goes with shark-fishing. I found him at his home in Bracara, a small crofting township perched high up on the north side of Loch Morar.

He was at that time twenty-five years old, a tall upright young fellow, with light-brown hair and merry, twinkling blue eyes. For his years he had had a wide and varied career, having started work in a Glasgow shipyard at the age of thirteen. He was an orphan and had a high regard for Miss Walker, who had brought him up from babyhood; many a son was not as good to his mother as Johnny was to her. At fifteen he returned to live in Bracara, doing all the seasonal work on her croft and tackling any odd job that came his way. He was much sought after as a fishing ghillie by the anglers who spend their holidays by Loch Morar. With his accurate knowledge of the habits and whereabouts of the trout and salmon, combined with his tireless energy when rowing a boat, he was worth his weight in gold to them. I have seen him driving a crane when they were building the hydro-electric scheme in Morar, and I have also seen him acting as Assistant Registrar doing the Census. Miss Walker was the District Registrar, and she was by then getting too old for such an active ploy as Census-taking.

He had worked in the woods as a lumberjack with Polish woodsmen in Morar, and I remember seeing him, shirtless and deeply tanned by the sun, and thinking that, whereas clothes make some men, the opposite was true of Johnny. He was very fond of horses, and I vividly recall one stalking season in Meoble forest, when he had taken the job of ponyman. He had been provided with three unbroken Highland ponies with which to pack the stags home; under anyone else's care their one aim and object seemed to be to get rid of the stag, anyhow, anywhere, as quickly as possible. Johnny must have been able to talk to these ponies in their own language, for they would follow him like dogs. To train unbroken ponies quickly is a task in itself, but to get them not only to approach a newly dead and frequently bloody carcase, let alone to carry it home willingly, is quite an achievement. He was equally at home at sea as in the mountains, for he often took a berth herring fishing in winter, or at the greatline or lobster fishing. He spent a great deal of his spare time reading, 'filling in the gaps in my education, Tex', he used to say. He did not drink, except on very special occasions when he might be persuaded to take a minute glass of liqueur whisky. As I expected he jumped at the chance of a season's sharkfishing but could not get away until he had finished his spring sowing, which he expected to do by the first few days of April.

I had the *Traveller* beached by Morar river and on 'legs' to keep her on an even keel, and she was by then painted outside and in. The engine was overhauled and a mast and derrick rigged; all that remained was the mounting of the gun. It was to be mounted on a tripod, the three legs of which were welded to a circle of steel plate, but as the deck sloped I would require to put a huge wedge-shaped block of wood between the gun mounting and the deck to level it off. It was some time before I managed to acquire a block of wood four feet long, three feet broad and a foot thick. Eventually we got our block and cut to shape for nothing or — should I say? — for services rendered to the Mallaig carpenter when Johnny and I helped him to man-handle some massive logs on to a lorry. As there was no recoil action on any of the guns, and remembering how the kick from old 'Sugan' used to make the deck leak, I put half a heavy motor tyre between the circle at the base of the tripod and the wedge before bolting down the gun mounting. To strengthen the gun mounting extra oak beams were fastened below it, one below the other, and all bolted together, for I felt that the single beams below the deck, although very strong, were insufficient. To give the gun the necessary freedom of movement we had it bolted into a crutch, the leg of which was made of two-inch diameter nickel-chrome steel, while the 'armrest' had high sides rather like a rowlock. The leg part of the crutch, being round, slewed in the gunmounting, and the bolt fastening the gun to the crutch gave us our up-and-down movement.

Without the harpoons I had bought from the old Soay Company or others identical, I knew that it would not have been worth my while attempting to catch sharks. They were the ultimate result of a great number of lengthy, frustrating and expensive experiments, the financial burden of which was borne entirely by Gavin Maxwell before the Soay Company came into being. The first harpoons we had fired from a gun were, in the light of greater experience, rather ridiculous, and so they progressed in design step by step until we arrived at these. Even so, it was not until we had the barbs made of hand-forged nickel-chrome steel that they could be trusted. The harpoon proper was an eighteen-inch-long shaft of inch-and-a-quarter-diameter steel turned down to a point like a well-sharpened pencil. There were two pairs of hinged barbs set at right-angles to each other, one at four and the other at six inches back from the point. There was a hole bored four inches from the butt end to take the wire with which we fastened the harpoons to the harpoon rope. The harpoon was fitted, by means of a steel sleeve, into an expendable hickory shaft three feet long. This shaft could be rammed down the barrel before putting on the harpoon when preparing for a shot; thus the business end of the harpoon was well clear of the barrel when about to fire at a fish. I liked these sticks because, unlike steel ones, they could be classed as a safety measure. Should a harpooned shark, when winched to the surface alongside the boat, have a foot or more of steel shaft sticking out of his back, he could drive it clean through the boat's bottom, with disastrous results. A shark always dives straight to the bottom immediately it is harpooned and there rolls, invariably breaking a wooden stick off flush with his back or getting rid of it altogether. Were the shaft to be made of steel and incorporated in the harpoon, he would most certainly bend it, rendering the harpoon useless until the shaft had been made absolutely straight again.

I bought several coils of three-and-a-half-inch rope, a coil being 120 fathoms, and some specially strong wire rope. The harpoon had to have a couple of fathoms of this wire spliced into it and to this was joined the harpoon rope, for obviously we could not bore a hole in a one-and-a-quarter-inch-diameter harpoon big enough to take a three-and-a-half-inch rope.

With my scheme to take the liver aboard at sea depending on the mast and derrick, I rigged several new pulley blocks that worked and re-stayed the mast with new wire, splicing it properly this time – the previous wires had more closely resembled the guys of a telegraph pole with attendant fittings rather than the stays of a boat's mast! As we had to allow for spending a week at least at sea, we made the fo'c'sle as comfortable as possible. We completely repainted it and I built a larger grub-locker, laid some lino on the floor and made a 'table', actually a piece of plywood shaped to fit between the two bunks, which could be removed when not in use. We also had a portable radio set and a fine coal stove that boasted an oven. We were ready to hoist our Blue Peter by the 4th of April, the earliest that I had ever been ready for sharks. I have always found that sharks caught during the early part of the season are much bigger than those caught later on, and yield a greater percentage of oil per ton of liver. To save unnecessary expense in hunting for the first shark of the year we waited in Mallaig until one of the many fishermen we had asked to keep a look-out for us reported the presence of sharks in the area. Each morning as the herring boats came in we went from boat to boat inquiring if anyone had seen a shark, but it was not until the eighth that we got an affirmative answer. Sammy Martin, the skipper of one of the finest lobster boats in the district, had met one that morning off Neist Lighthouse, the most westerly point of Skye. In feverish haste we made ready to be off, first of all bringing aboard all those last-minute things, fresh meat, water and tobacco, and rechecking all our stores to make certain we should not go to sea without all we needed. To cope with any emergency I put aboard a large chest of tools and a vice, in fact sufficient gear to stock a decent garage – so much so that we were later to acquire the reputation of being a floating workshop, much in demand on the fishing grounds.

When at last we were ready Jeanne came down the pier, bringing the baby, whom we had called Duncan, to see us away. We had Jeanne let go our mooring ropes, for it is said to be lucky to have a fair-headed person do this for you when putting to sea. There is a tremendous amount of superstition among the older fishermen about this, dark-headed women being absolutely taboo, while to mention pigs, rabbits or clergymen of any denomination when leaving the harbour is thought to bring disaster. Newly painted, our little boat looked clean and spruce and I felt proud of her that day. She did not remain long in this condition, for a few sharks soon made havoc of all our efforts to make her look like a yacht.

It was a lovely day with clear blue sky and not a breath of wind. Soon we were chugging merrily across the sound towards Sleat Point with its small automatic lighthouse. Away ahead one sees the mountainous island deer forest, Rum, and south of it the smaller but more populated island of Eigg. The latter I am afraid I shall never really like, being unable to forget the night it afforded me such unfriendly anchorage. Rounding Sleat Point we could see below the magnificent peaks of the Cuillins the tiny isle of Soay and from then onwards we could also see the island of Canna, the most friendly and fertile island of the group. I shall always associate Canna with birds, for the cliffs on the east side are densely populated by puffins, guillemots, razorbills and many other seabirds. Eider ducks are often to be seen sunning themselves on the little concrete jetty just below the proprietor's house. They are so tame that one can walk right up to them, for they know they have nothing to fear there. At the wish of John Lorne Campbell, who owns the island, it is treated as a bird sanctuary and no firearms of any sort are allowed. This ban on firearms prompted me to ask permission to fire my harpoon gun in the anchorage. This obtained, I was later to catch several sharks right in front of Mr Campbell's house.

On our way to Soay Johnny disappeared below and it was not long before smoke was curling from the fo'c'sle chimney; his intentions soon became obvious with the smell of frying kippers wafting through the open hatch. Shortly afterwards an arm appeared through the hatch and laid a plate on deck; this was followed by another and a teapot, a couple of mugs and the necessary eating irons before Johnny himself emerged, shirtless and complaining of the heat in the fo'c'sle. This welcome meal we ate off the top of the wheelhouse, which was just the right height to allow us to do this and still steer the boat with our feet. She was steered by a tiller, the wheelhouse having no wheel, nor a back, being a three-sided shelter for the helmsman. When we had finished eating, we leaned against the wheelhouse, smoking luxuriously and drinking in the scenery away ahead. I do not know a more wonderful panorama than that which opened before us on rounding Sleat Point as we steamed straight for the towering peaks of the Cuillins. One often sees postcard views of them but this before us, so much more worth recording than many of the others, never seems to be among them. Could it be that professional photographers suffer from seasickness? I thought of the expensive luxury cruises where people actually paid to do this sort of thing, and did not acquire half as good a tan as Johnny and I sported at the end of the season. We even had our sun-tan oil thrown in, often literally. Wonderful stuff, shark liver!

I did not like to pass Soay and held the *Traveller* straight into the village bay. There we met Ronald Macdonald of the *Hetty*, who came out in his dinghy to meet us. As he had seen no sharks around Soay so far that year, we did not stay very long. We had quite a distance to go before reaching Neist Point and in the hope of meeting a shark on the way there we followed the Skye shore across the mouth of Loch Brittle and on past Loch Eynort and

Loch Bracadale, places where I had caught a good number of sharks when employed by the old Soay Company. We reached Moonen Bay, the north end of which terminates in Neist Point with its essential lighthouse, without having seen a shark. We cruised round slowly for an hour or so with a similar lack of success and, as it was by then past sunset and would soon be dark, we decided to tie up for the night at the lighthouse jetty. Before doing this, however, we fished for cod until we caught sufficient to go round the lighthouse-keepers' families, for I knew they had no boat and were only able to fish off the rocks. This fish was gratefully received when we later visited the lighthouse in search of news of sharks. During the season we became great friends with the keepers, to whom we were a welcome diversion from the usual monotony which is the lot of such isolated outposts. The odd feed of fish with which we managed to supply them was more than amply repaid by their services as shark-spotters. They took an active interest which proved exceedingly helpful, for a keeper looking down from his high vantage point could spot a shark cruising just beneath the surface and indicate its position to us far below. That evening they told us that they had seen a shark the previous morning just below the light and that later in the evening he was seen again, feeding on the surface in Moonen Bay. Whether this was the same fish or not, they could not tell, so we went to our bunks in high hopes of meeting a shark in the morning.

Next morning we were abroad bright and early, the day promising to be as fine as its predecessor. After we had eaten our breakfast, Johnny loaded the gun with meticulous care; I think he almost counted the grains of gunpowder before declaring everything to be ready. All day long we cruised along the shore, up and down and in and out, without seeing a single shark. We were afraid to go far away from the lighthouse in any direction, feeling sure that the shark would appear the moment we had left. About four o'clock we felt we had had enough and set the sail, there being by now a light breeze of nor-east wind, and started off across the

Minch. I had learned from experience that sharks invariably appear first in this area about Barra at the southern end of the Outer Hebrides. We were only about 500 yards off the light when, looking back the way we had come, I saw a gannet diving for fish. I can never tire of watching these beautiful snow-white birds as they fold their wings and drop from a great height straight as a dart for the fish they must see below the surface. We fishermen have found that a gannet dives vertically when fishing for herring, and diagonally and from much less height when fishing for mackerel, with its wings not quite closed, ready until the last moment to change direction before entering the water. This gannet was behaving as if it was fishing for herring, and both herring and basking sharks are plankton feeders. So round I went to have one last look. I hoped that the concentration of plankton might rise nearer the surface, bringing the shark up with it, should one be there.

Johnny, standing by the gun, which was by then unloaded and covered as we did not want to get it wet with spray while crossing the Minch, saw the fin first. The gannet dived almost on top of it. Johnny cheered lustily and shouted: 'See him, Tex?'

But I, too, had been watching the gannet. The cover was quickly whipped off and the gun reloaded. The harpoon rope was hauled up and reshackled to the wire in the harpoon and we were ready for him. As we closed with the fish, Johnny came aft to take over the helm from me but I wanted him to try the first shot himself. He did not want to do this in case he would miss.

'What of it?' I said. 'We've all missed, even the best of us, and I'm sure I can handle the boat better than you can, and I'll guarantee to put you within ten yards of his back. You aim for just aft and slightly to one side of the dorsal fin, then pull the trigger and leave the rest to "Sugan". Don't fire too soon; wait until you're right up to him, but fire if he begins to go down. When we get up close to the shark I won't be able to see him, so signal with your hand which way you want me to go.'

Rather reluctantly he took his place at the gun while I went in close to the fish. We approached the shark from the rear and at the last moment I swung out and away from him, putting the boat on the same parallel: this gives the man at the gun a clear view of the whole shark and enables him to place his harpoon better. The shark was a beauty, almost thirty feet long, and as I drew nearer I could see his great broad back, for all the world like a small blue-grey submarine, with its decks just awash. The tip of his nose and the top half of his tail were often well clear of the water and the colossal dorsal fin flopped over at the top with its own weight. His huge white mouth was wide open as he fed on the millions of minute marine plants and animals collectively called plankton.

Suddenly Johnny was waving me frantically away from the shark and the gun went off with a great roar, followed almost immediately by an almighty wallop on the boat's side and for a moment Johnny was lost in a shower of spray. The harpoon rope began to sing out, springing out of its coils like a snake, only to be straightened out quicker than the eye could follow and away over the side, out through the rollers in her stem. I shouted to Johnny to get out of the way of the rope, but he seemed to be in a daze, just standing there holding on to the gun, and I knocked the engine out of gear in case our forward way should carry us over the shark and our propeller pick up the harpoon rope. I sprang from the wheel-house, ran forward and made the harpoon rope fast to the forward samson post, but only with a couple of round turns, in case we should need to give him more line. This sudden activity on my part seemed to bring Johnny to life and he rushed to help me.

'God, Tex!' he said, 'you were right when you said pull the trigger and leave the rest to "Sugan", for as we got up to him, the shark suddenly rushed at us, crossed our stem, and dived beneath the boat. I could only see his tail when I fired. I aimed for where I figured his back to be, took a chance and pulled the trigger. But when he lashed out at us with that terrific tail, I thought we'd had it.'

Despite the round turns on the samson post our combined strength was insufficient to hold the shark and we were forced to pay out rope at an alarming rate. We had lost about sixty fathoms by the time we had it fast.

During this time we were being towed slowly ahead, but as soon as we made fast the boat quickly gathered way as the shark headed for the open sea. I could not judge the speed at which the shark towed us along, but it far exceeded anything we could attain under our own power, although the initial rush lasted only five minutes. The shark quickly slowed down and soon we were moving so slowly ahead that, had it not been so calm, our bow wave would not have been visible. Leaving the shark to tow us where he would and so tire himself out a bit, I went below and made a cup of tea.

Nothing would persuade Johnny to come off the deck, so I brought the mugs and some bread and jam and joined him by the gun. I shall always remember vividly the picture of Johnny, shirtless, sitting at the stem of the boat, a large chunk of bread and jam in his left hand while with his right he endeavoured to feel the strain on the rope and hold his mug of tea at the same time.

By this time we were hardly moving at all, for the shark, finding himself in deeper water, was trying to get to the bottom, and therefore the strain on the rope was such that I was certain that it would be useless to attempt to winch him to the surface.

We contemplated giving him sufficient rope to allow him to get to the bottom, feeling sure that, once he realised he could not rid himself of the harpoon, he would set off for the open sea again, towing the boat behind him. Those who have foul-hooked a salmon (i.e. through the back) will appreciate the colossal power of a basking shark, weighing upwards of five tons, and the terrific strain on the rope while the fish bores straight down trying to get to the bottom. If he would only move ahead again, drawing the boat after him, it would certainly lessen the strain. The shark, however, was not on our side and refused to oblige, so we were forced to let him have all the rope he wanted in order to get to the bottom, for we felt sure that the rope was rapidly approaching breaking point.

Soon we were being towed slowly ahead, but this time shore-wards. Gulping down the remains of our tea, we cleared the deck and made ready to winch him back. Johnny, still sitting in the bows feeling his harpoon line, shouted: 'Look Tex, another one!'

I looked up from my task and, following his outstretched arm, saw, away in shore, a few hundred yards from where we had har-pooned the shark we were fast to, the unmistakable black dorsal fin of another fish. Hurrying forward I leaned over the stem to feel the strain on the harpoon rope. It was as straight as a bar and every bit as stiff.

'Let's load the gun while we still have time,' I said, 'for I am going to play a trick on him, and if it works we'll have him on the surface a damn sight quicker than he would come of his own free will, and anyway if it doesn't work we'll at least have tired him out a bit.' I explained to Johnny that I had always wanted to reverse the process, and instead of allowing the shark to tow us around until he got tired, why didn't we tow him until we got tired?

I had every faith in the rope and harpoon if the latter was embedded properly in the fish, but neither Johnny nor I had any idea where the harpoon was. Long ago I had made a vow never to treat a shark as one should play a trout – fearing that the harpoon might come out – for in the days of the Soay Company when fishing from the little *Gannet*, here in Moonen Bay, I had har-pooned seven sharks one after another, hauling each one of them laboriously hand-over-hand, only to lose them all as I got each one to the surface. Of course this was before we had the harpoons made of nickel-chrome steel. We both agreed that if we were going to lose the shark it was better to do so at the start, more especially so when there was another one to be seen on the surface.

With the harpoon rope still fast to the forward samson post we passed the free end, double, down the starboard side, outboard of the forestay and the starboard stay, making the part with the shark attached fast to the samson post aft; the other part (that is, the free end) led back to the main coil just aft of the mast. We then steamed full speed ahead into the harpoon rope and this gave us sufficient slack to untie it from the stem and clear it from the stemhead roller. As soon as the rope was clear of the stem I took the engine out of gear and waited for the shark to tow us by the stern. We had not long to wait before we were off, seawards, though not very fast, maybe three or four knots, by the stern.

So far, so good. We cautiously put the engine into ahead but this made no difference, the shark having gathered momentum when we helped him by going ahead to slacken the line. By now the harpoon rope was leading almost perpendicularly down and we imagined he had reached the bottom, although we were still going astern. We gradually gave her more throttle until the engine was going all out. There was a great turmoil at her propeller but we were still going astern. The shark maintained this state of affairs for about a quarter of an hour while Johnny, standing at her stem, threw matches over the side in an effort to judge our speed. Soon it was checkmate, neither side progressing, and Johnny must have used most of his box of matches before shouting: 'We're gaining, Tex! The matches are going astern of us.'

It was only then that I noticed that the rope was not leading down at such a steep angle; we were towing him up. We both glued our eyes to the rope, fascinated as more and more of it came in sight until it was almost straight astern of us. Should I live to be a hundred I shall never forget the spectacle of that first shark I ever towed to the surface. First his head reared out of the water, like some prehistoric monster seen in a nightmare, and then disappeared beneath the surface in a great swirl of foam, to be followed by his huge tail which hung poised momentarily in the air, before slapping down on the water with a report like gun-fire, which could be heard above our exultant roars. Johnny clasped both hands above his head like a triumphant boxer, danced a step or two and disappeared down the engine-room hatch as if the devil was after him, shouting: 'We've won, Tex!'

Thinking there was something wrong with the engine, I looked down to see what he was up to and laughed to see him, an oil-can

in one hand, patting the engine with the other, as he oiled everything he could think of, and shouting above the noise of the
engine: 'Good on you, lassie! You've beaten the bastard!'

I remember thinking that we had not exactly beaten him yet,
and that it is a good thing that a shark has little brain, for Heaven
help us if he knew how to use his colossal strength.

We towed him thus, right into the middle of the bay, which
took us, I think, maybe another ten minutes, and then prepared to
winch him alongside. This is quite a tricky business, for a shark,
although obviously tired out, can still do a tremendous amount of
damage, with his tail lashing out in every direction, when he is
brought alongside the boat. We put the winch into top gear and
hauled him up towards our stem, the rope being by now locked in
the stemhead roller again. With the aid of the winch one man has
to keep the shark as close to the boat as possible while the other
tries to lasso the tail when it comes out of the water. At this time
the tail often comes aboard. I do not believe that the shark is
deliberately trying to do any damage; he is merely lashing out in
an effort to get away. I warned Johnny to be more than careful
when lassoing it, but I might as well have saved my breath. Several
times Johnny merely ducked or dodged, allowing the tail to come
slapping down on the rail inches from him. I felt sure that one of
these times the shark would get him, and if he were to go over the
side between the shark and the boat that tail would flatten him
like a pancake. After a great many frustrating near-misses he at last
managed to throw the lasso over the tail, and we had him.

He passed the end of the lasso back to me at the winch and,
taking off the harpoon rope, I heaved the tail right up to the stem,
clean out of the water, and shouted to Johnny to set the engine
away half-speed ahead. This naturally brought the shark tight
alongside. We were then able to see that the harpoon had passed
clean through the fish about a foot aft of the dorsal fin and that my
first guess at a length of thirty feet was near enough, for the shark's
head almost reached the stern.

The weight of the shark gave us quite a list to port and this helped us to stick a grinda-hook with a rope attached into his lower jaw. We both heaved with all our might until we had the head as tight alongside as was possible. During this time the boat steered herself. I had put the helm to starboard and we were going round in circles to port which kept the shark tight alongside, but we made very little actual headway. Towing him this way, tail first, all his fins seemed to get in the way of the water, and his five sets of gills, which almost completely encircle the head, opened out like five great, ugly sea-anchors which caught a tremendous amount of water.

We could still see the other shark on the surface, cruising near the shore and quite oblivious of his cousin's desperate plight, and this made us work fast as we set about what Johnny used to call 'de-livering'. First of all we removed the harpoon, and as it had passed right through the fish this was easy, we only had to lean over the side and pull it aboard, unshackling it where the harpoon wire joins the rope. We pulled the rope aboard, out through his back. My scheme for getting the liver aboard at sea depended entirely upon what the local herring-men call a 'brailer'. This is an outsize edition of a trout-landing net, with an eight-foot pole as a handle, and the hoop at the mouth end of the net three feet six inches in diameter. The net is in the shape of a fool's cap, fifteen feet deep, with a rope attached to the peak of the cap which runs through a block at the top of the derrick, through another block at the foot of the mast, and back to the winch, the derrick, of course, being swung out to extend just over the side. We could cut open the shark from the deck by means of a large knife blade fitted into a six-foot pole. The first cut we made across the shark as near his throat as the pectoral fins would allow, and the second cut longitudinally from aft of the vent right up to meet the first cut. As soon as this was complete, out came the liver of its own accord, helped of course by our forward way, its high oil content naturally causing it to float. We scooped about a quarter of the liver into the brail-net, the depth of the net allowing us to lift the pole and hoop aboard without taking the weight of the liver. The hoop we placed vertically, tight against the rail. There was a rope with a small steel hook on the end tied to the other side of the boat, and this hook we stuck in at the top of the hoop to keep it from falling backwards over the side. By heaving on the winch the rope attached to the end of the net we hove the latter up to the derrick and the liver slid down on to the deck where we cut it into sizeable chunks and packed it into barrels. We repeated this operation until all the liver was aboard, filling seven barrels which we estimated at about fourteen hundred weights. Without further ado we got rid of him and, taking the lasso off his tail and the hook out of his jaw, I watched him slowly sink astern before dashing to the wheelhouse and setting off full-speed for the other shark.

I felt very pleased with myself for, ever since I had removed the liver from a very small shark with the aid of a dinghy and a bucket in Harris, while fishing with the old Soay Company, I had felt that it could be done at sea in reasonable weather, and if we were lucky enough to catch one in bad weather we could always tow it to the nearest shelter and work it there; now I had proved it.

In retrospect the time, fuel and temper we expended in the early days towing, say, four sharks at a time, up to a hundred miles back to the factory at Soay, was simply ridiculous, for it gained us nothing and sent the overheads soaring. When later we had progressed to beaching the fish and removing the liver there, we may have saved some fuel but very little time, and for my part certainly no temper. Consider that the best we ever did in those days with Maxwell's two boats and nine men was twelve sharks caught in one day, the total number for that week was twenty, and it took us the best part of the next week to get their livers into barrels and the carcases towed away. Furthermore those boats were quite incapable of carrying their own cargo and had to have a 'puffer' to carry that liver to Soay.

The best day's fishing Johnny and I had with the *Traveller* was eight sharks.

Chapter Four

That same week we left Mallaig at 4 a.m. on Monday morning and caught the first shark at midday; leaving the fishing grounds at 11 p.m., we were back in Mallaig the following morning before six, where we discharged our liver and took on more empty barrels, clearing out to sea at once again. It was a great week, the engine was running non-stop from Monday morning until late Saturday night.

This second shark seemed to be on sentry duty for he was cruising quite close to the shore, up and down an area several hundred yards long, seeming always to turn at the same point of both ends of his beat. We reached him just as he turned to go away from us and, easing down the engine, gradually overtook him. Just before he was due to turn again, Johnny let him have it. It was a long shot, as long a shot as I have ever tried with such a heavy harpoon rope. As the harpoon reached him I was amazed to see the fish suddenly stop dead and remain motionless for several seconds. This time Johnny acted at once and, jumping for the main part of the harpoon rope, had it fast with the usual round turns before I had the engine out of gear. Our forward way brought us right up close to him and I could clearly see the wire just below his dorsal fin and a little trickle of dark blood, but no sign of the harpoon.

When he did move he moved like greased lightning away seawards on the surface like a torpedo; I imagine there was not enough water so close to the shore for him to dive. Since he had stopped dead immediately he was harpooned he had not taken much rope and the next minute the boat was almost pulled over, for she was not pointing the way the shark was going; there was a fearful jerk and the boat's bows were pulled down and sideways at the same time and before we were round in line with the shark we had scooped aboard quite a lot of water. We quickly let him have about eighty fathoms of rope – or perhaps I should say he took it – for even supposing we had tried it is unlikely that we could have held it.

Away we went with a fair turn of speed, clear out of the bay, where even the strong tide-race which flows round Neist Point did nothing to retard our progress, although it certainly would have, had we been under our own power. As we passed below the lighthouse I looked up to see the three keepers out on the 'pulpit', obviously cheering us on, one of them waving a telescope round and round his head, but Johnny and I were unable to return the salute for we were both sitting on the foredeck with our feet braced against something, holding on to the harpoon rope behind the round turns on the samson post in fear of losing the lot. We certainly were a diversion and the keepers were later to tell me that they had prayed for a cine-camera, for from their high vantage point they apparently could not only see the shark just beneath the surface but the rope leading from it straight to the stem of the *Traveller*, and boring the tide, which was dead against us, we appeared to be going much faster than we actually were. Luckily the shark did not maintain this speed for long, and as soon as he had eased down sufficiently we were able to make the rope fast properly. I don't know how Johnny felt, but I was sure my arms were inches longer. Out clear of the tide-race the shark turned and towed us in a southerly direction, parallel with the land, maybe a mile offshore, and very soon slowed down, and we got on with the business of towing him to the surface. This fellow behaved rather well and, as Johnny had got the hang of things, we were much quicker in dealing with him, but he yielded only six barrels although he was just as big.

They were both male sharks and I therefore figured there

ought to be some females in the vicinity, for I have never experienced a shoal of sharks all of the same sex. After we were clear of this fish I went below to demonstrate my culinary prowess with some tomato soup, a tin of bully-beef and a can-opener, leaving Johnny to steer the boat and keep a sharp look-out. I was just about to bring this up on deck as Johnny had done for me when he began to roar, calling me up on deck, and the engine leapt into full speed. Thinking something terrible had happened, I dropped everything and popped my head out of the hatch.

'What's up, Johnny?' I cried.

'Sharks! Sharks, Tex! Dozens of them, away in by the lighthouse jetty,' he shouted. Scuttling aft, I took over the helm, the meal forgotten, while Johnny ran to the gun. There must have been a score of fins showing at one time, so closely packed that I thought the fish must be ramming each other as they cruised slowly round and round in a very small area. In a matter of seconds Johnny gave me the thumbs-up signal, indicating that the gun was loaded and the harpoon ready. I eased the engine down to dead slow and cautiously approached them, hoping I would not ram one as I reached the outer edge of their circle. There was one huge fish, darker and much larger than the rest, his dorsal fin was so tall that it lay over at an angle, like a sailing boat with a broken mast.

'Try for the big one with the floppy fin,' I shouted to Johnny as we drew near. We had to wait outside the circle until the big fellow drew abreast of us and, when we got our chance, I quickly slipped up beside him. We were only about ten feet from his back when Johnny pulled the trigger, but 'Sugan' did not give her usual roar, instead she merely farted, at least that is how it sounded to me, and the harpoon simply fell out of the gun. The shark paid not the slightest attention to us but continued on his way, following the rest of the pack in their perambulations. The expression on Johnny's face was really comical – a mixture of indignation, dismay and shocked surprise. I could do nothing other than roar with laughter and swing the boat out of the way of the sharks in case one of them should do us damage. Knocking her out of gear,

I went forward to see what had happened. My first thought was that Johnny had made some mistake in the excitement, either forgetting to put in a wad, or not putting in enough powder when he loaded the gun.

'I couldn't have had a better chance,' he said. 'The harpoon was almost touching his back when I pulled the trigger, but the bloody gun only fizzed like a damp squib.' And we both laughed when I told him how it had sounded to me. On inspection we found that the wooden harpoon shaft had split and half of it was still in the barrel. When I later told this to a gunmaker he said it was a wonder the barrel did not split, but old 'Sugan' was made of good stuff. To make things more awkward, the stick had split diagonally and all we could feel was the sharp point of it about eight inches from the muzzle. 'Sugan' had had it until we could get this shaft out.

'Let's have it off, Johnny, and screw on Maxwell's gun. If we're quick we'll maybe get another go.'

This gun was exactly the same size as 'Sugan', only the bolt holding it to the crutch in the gun mounting was much larger, so we had to dismantle the mounting and fit another crutch. This took us longer than we had anticipated and by the time we were ready all the sharks had submerged. We cruised about the bay until it was almost dark, but saw no more sharks that evening. A fresh breeze of southerly wind had sprung up, so we made for Pooltiel, the next loch north of us, where we would be more comfortable lying at anchor than bumping all night against the lighthouse jetty, which is exposed to this wind. By the time we were snug at our anchor in Loch Pooltiel it had started to rain and the wind had increased to half a gale; we were glad to get below and close the hatch. We stoked up the stove and turned on the wireless before opening the medicine box that we always carried aboard but never needed; producing our bottle of whisky, we drank a toast to our success and to the speedy recovery of Sugan's health, but how we were to remove the obstruction from her throat neither of us knew.

Chapter Four

'Let's sleep on it, Johnny,' I said at last, for I was pleasantly tired, my belly was full and I had a warm bunk.

We awoke next morning to a howling gale and the early weather forecast did not promise us any immediate improvement. So after breakfast we brought old 'Sugan' into the fo'c'sle and laid her on the table to begin our efforts to get the stick out.

The Martini action which fires a .38 blank, together with the manipulating handle, could be screwed off, leaving just the barrel. Inserting a piece of wire up the .38 breech we measured eight inches before we met the shaft, but it was not all there, some of it must have gone over the side with the harpoon. I found that I could blow through the barrel, so the wad we ram home behind the main charge was damaged, if there at all. As we could not load the gun properly, that is, from the muzzle end, we would require to try and load it from the other end, but first of all we would have to get some sort of wad in place before we were able to fire out what remained of the shaft. We tore up a whole newspaper that we had got from the lighthouse keepers a couple of nights before and poked it all through the .38 breech with our wire, but still we could blow through the barrel. We tried rags and oakum, jabbing and poking away with our wire in our efforts to make the barrel airtight before we could pour in the gunpowder, all to no avail. I spent hours with the wire, prodding in every direction I could, but failed absolutely to make the barrel airtight. All sorts of ideas were thought up only to be discarded as impracticable by one or other of us, until Johnny had the best idea of all – some hot pitch poured down the barrel was bound to bung everything up when it cooled ... but we had no pitch. Hours later I was sitting on Johnny's bunk on the opposite side of the fo'c'sle from the grub-locker and drinking a mug of tea, when Johnny opened the door to get some biscuits, and I could see there, just inside, was our answer. Johnny had included it in our grocery order, 'just for an emergency', he said. If ever there was an emergency, this was certainly one, I thought. As Johnny turned and handed me the biscuits I held his gaze for a moment or two before whispering the magic word 'POM'. It took only a second for the penny to drop and he broke into a gleeful grin.

'The very thing, Tex!' he said. His grin was no doubt largely occasioned by the disparaging remarks I had made when he brought it aboard, for I, like many other soldiers, was familiar only with the 'goo' which resulted from its ill-treatment by Army cooks.

We put the kettle on the stove and made a funnel out of a sheet of writing paper; then, turning 'Sugan' upside down, gently poured about half the potato powder down behind our newspapers and oakum. We inserted a pencil to see how much room was left between the Pom and the .38 breech, estimating two inches. As soon as the kettle was boiling we followed that up with some boiling water and propped old 'Sugan' against a bunk and left her like that for an hour to give the Pom plenty of time to swell. We then added a little more in the hope of drying up any remaining dampness, then we huffed, and we puffed, but we couldn't blow the Pom down. Since that day I have always meant to write a letter of thanks to the manufacturers of this excellent product, but perhaps some of them may read these lines.

We measured the eight drams of gunpowder to follow up the Pom and, discovering that it would not hold any more, we inserted a spent cartridge stuffed with newspaper to keep the powder in before screwing on the Martini action. It did not take us long to change over the crutch and mount 'Sugan'. In case anything went wrong – that is, should the barrel burst – we tied a long string to the trigger and both went down into the hold.

One, two, three . . . and I pulled the string. The gun went off with a tremendous bang, quite different from the usual roar, scaring all the seagulls which had gathered round the boat when we had thrown the remains of our breakfast over the side. I often try to imagine the reactions in the scattered croft houses within earshot round the lochside, when their occupants heard, first the explosion, and then our blood-curdling yells of triumph when we discovered that old 'Sugan' had cleared her throat.

It had been raining hard when we came on deck to change the

crutch but it had by now stopped and as the wind had dropped we were itching to see if the pack of sharks we had met the previous evening was still in Moonen Bay. So we started up, heaved in the anchor and went out to have a look. Clear of the shelter of the loch we found there was still a fresh breeze blowing, so we had very little hope of doing much about it, even if we should sight them. Going round Neist Point we encountered very heavy seas, for the wind was against the ebb tide. On reaching Moonen Bay the sea was such that it would have been impossible to hold a shark alongside, and it was questionable if we could allow the boat to become broadside on.

There was nothing for it but to turn back and content our-selves until the weather moderated, so rather reluctantly we returned to our anchorage without seeing a single fin.

The following morning the wind had gone, so back we went to Moonen Bay in search of the sharks. We did not meet them as a pack again but by the end of the week we had met and caught another three sharks, one of which was small, before steaming home, where we landed twenty-nine barrels of shark liver, our first catch of the season.

On Saturday morning, while we were unloading our cargo at Mallaig, several herring men came to tell us that there were quite a number of large sharks at Tarbert Bay at the south end of the island of Canna, and that some of the boats had had their nets torn by them. The fishermen were all keen that we should shift our hunting ground and try and rid them of the brutes.

As there was a tremendous number of ring-net boats in harbour preparing for sea, as is usual on a Monday morning, each one taking aboard stores, water, fuel, etc., we were rather late in getting to sea for we found ourselves far down the waiting list for the oil-merchant's tanker. It was well on in the day before we were under way, and 7 p.m. before we reached Canna.

We were just off Canna Lighthouse, in the sound between the islands of Rum and Canna, when a large shark suddenly surfaced about 500 yards ahead of us and began to disport himself in a most spectacular manner. He appeared to be turning somersaults, for one minute we could see him swimming high on the surface with the tip of his nose and most of his dorsal fin and tail well clear of the water. Next he appeared to dive vertically, thrusting his tail and almost a third of his length high into the air, only to bring it slapping down on the water with a tremendous splash. It was these splashes which drew my attention in the first place.

As we drew nearer the splashes grew less frequent and we were about 100 yards off him when he stopped his antics and began to behave more normally, swimming lazily on the surface, away from us. On closer inspection he appeared to be lighter in colour than the fish we had caught in Moonen Bay. I have often noticed this, not that there were always lighter-coloured fish in Canna, but there seemed to be distinct families which we thought we could recognize. Certainly for instance some 'families' had more white on their bellies than had others.

The ring-net men had certainly not been romancing when they reported large sharks, for this fellow was all of thirty feet and gave the impression of having the girth of an elephant. We kept going all out, straight for the fish. Johnny seemed to take a maddeningly long time to fire the gun. It always seems like that to the man at the tiller, but in actual fact the longer the harpoonier can hold his fire with his sights trained on the shark's back, the better the shot he is likely to make. We must have been less than ten feet from his back when Johnny fired the harpoon, our forward way carrying us right up on top of him. As I took the engine out of gear I felt the boat strike the shark and mount his back, list and slip off. Next instant the shark seemed to explode, and the *Traveller* was literally battered out of the way. Lashing out with his tail he struck us several hefty wallops, showering the boat and drenching both Johnny and me with spray before he condescended to sound. The harpoon rope shot out of its coils and before we had it fast he had taken 150 fathoms in as many seconds.

'Lively bastard that, Tex!' Johnny remarked. 'What say we have a cuppa before we begin to work him?'

'Good idea,' I replied, 'but we'll give him some more line. We'll give him 200 fathoms. He'll need it here. One of the deepest holes in the area is just ahead of us.'

Despite his aquabatic display he did not tow us very fast, no more than two or three knots, when we gave him his 200 fathoms. When we thought everything was under control, Johnny went below to make the tea and I to the engine room to stop the engine, as it was impossible to engage the winch pulley which drove the winch belt when the engine was running. We always disengaged this pulley on passage, for we believed it helped our speed. I did not restart the engine but hurried forward in answer to Johnny's shout of: 'Come and get it!'

The shark must have been sulking for he had not towed us more than 100 yards by the time we went aft to start the engine. This old engine started on petrol, and only when the vaporizer was hot enough could it be switched to paraffin. Finding that the little petrol squirt for priming the cylinders was empty, I handed it up on deck for Johnny to fill from a five-gallon drum which we carried on deck aft of the wheelhouse, together with some spare tins of paraffin. With the squirt full I primed the cylinders; I cranked and I cursed and cranked again, but no sign of life. We put a piece of pipe over the starting handle to lengthen it and we cranked together, Johnny on one side and I on the other, winding away for all we were worth, but no amount of winding would start the engine. We checked everything we could think of, even re-timed the magneto, but nothing seemed to be wrong and yet we could not get her to start; not even a splutter could we get out of her. I am afraid that the air in the engine room was blue. We took turns during the time we spent cranking to go up on deck and ascertain whether our 'anchor' was still holding, or should I say whether we still had a hold of the anchor. Soon a heavy drizzle had set in and it quickly grew dark, although the sea was as calm as a millpond. To complicate matters, the cut-out on our dynamo had jammed and when I had stopped the engine I had not noticed that the dynamo had 'motored back', draining the life out of the batteries and leaving us without lights. By this time we could see no sign of land but we did not think the shark would put us ashore as he drew as much water as the boat did, and anyway a harpooned shark invariably makes for the open sea. Luckily we had a Tilley lamp which we brought up on deck whenever we could see the lights of another boat. Our main worry was that we might be run down, as we were in an area much frequented by the herring boats, let alone trawlers and passing cargo boats.

Five long hours later, my head in my hands, completely beaten, I got it. My hands smelt of paraffin. I tried the squirt – also paraffin. Then I remembered. I had brought aboard a tin of petrol that morning but I had filled a green one and it was our usual habit to have petrol in a red tin. In our hurry to put to sea I had forgotten to warn Johnny of the switch-over and now felt like a fool. Priming the cylinders with petrol, we soon got the engine started. There is a feeling of life in a boat when the engine is running and the lights blazing, and with rising spirits we came on deck. We could see the lights of several herring boats away astern, but now that we had all our deck lights there was no fear of being run down. Making certain that the shark was still on, we went below for a much needed cup of tea. Johnny had a good fire in the fo'c'sle which he felt we needed on such a 'dreich' night, for we were tired and cold, now that the reaction had set in. I cannot now remember if I ever drank any of the tea, but I know I never finished it for I woke up in broad daylight, still sitting in my bunk. Johnny was still sitting in his, sound asleep, his elbow in the butter, his head resting on the fo'c'sle table and his mug untouched beside him.

A glance at the time showed me it was six o'clock. Still half asleep I bolted on to the deck and was relieved to see that not only were we still afloat, but we were still tied to our shark. Johnny, awakened by the racket I had made with my leather seaboots as I scuttled up on deck, quickly followed me.

'Where are we?' he asked.

'Round the corner, and the next land's America,' I replied. The shark had been a wonderful anchor but had towed us right across the Minch, clear of all the reefs and rocks, of which there is no shortage in the area. We were just south of Barra Head Lighthouse and as the morning was thick it was the only land we could see. The engine was still running, so everything was under control.

'Let's have another go at making tea, Tex, but you try your luck this time!'

The stove had gone out in the night but I soon had the Primus going and we made up in breakfast what we had lacked in supper.

As he had been towing the *Traveller* all night, we thought it unnecessary to give the shark any rough treatment. Surely he would be tired by now. We were wrong in this for he proved very obstinate; acting as a sea-anchor for us apparently had not worried him in the least. The extra strain as we heaved on the winch must have annoyed the fish for he turned us round about and set off, at a fair speed, back the way we had come. By putting the engine into gear we gained a lot of rope, nevertheless it was quite a struggle before we got him to come to the surface. There he was reluctant to remain, and lashed out in all directions with his tail in his frantic efforts to get away. We were forced to give him more line in case he should damage the boat, and gave him some extra weight by putting the engine into reverse. At last we got him alongside, but his tail-lashing was such that it was impossible for Johnny to get a lasso on his tail, for at times three-parts of the shark was clear of the water. Johnny, having lost his temper, was showering curses on the shark, 'his sisters, and his cousins and his aunts'. At last in rage, flinging down the lasso, he retaliated by lashing out at it with a cleaver the next time the tail came aboard. The cleaver was kept handy by the gunmounting in case it was necessary to cut away a shark in a hurry. I was beginning to wonder if the winch would be torn out of the deck by one of the sudden jerks, as the shark came half out of the water, and was about to let him sound again when we could give him a little towing medicine to cool him down a bit. I was too late. Without the slightest warning the winch belt broke and away went the shark, like a shot from a gun, faster than I had ever seen anything travel in the sea before, although he remained on the surface for less than a 100 yards before he sounded. As I had forgotten to throw over the ratchet which would have prevented the winch barrel from spinning free I had no control over the rope. Luckily Johnny was to starboard of the mast and did not get caught up in it. Somehow we managed to get the end fast and I dashed for the wheelhouse. Johnny was to warn me when the rope was almost all out, when I could set the boat ahead full speed to lessen the jerk as the rope came tight. I once had half the stem pulled out of a smaller boat with this same caper in the days of the old Soay Company. We must have timed it well for we felt very little jerk. All we could do was put the engine on astern full speed in an effort to tire him out a bit.

The winch belt was beyond repair at sea for it needed a new piece put in which we did not then have, although later we carried a complete spare belt. The only thing for it now was to haul the shark up by hand, and a long and tedious job it was, but we were greatly assisted by the swell, which allowed us to gain some slack on our downward swoop. Three hours later we had him on the surface and the first time he lifted his tail Johnny stuck the grinda-hook into the base of it. We had prepared the grinda-hook for this by lashing it to a boat-hook and this was the best grip we could hope for without a winch. We managed to get the tail hove pretty close up and the shark soon quietened down as the *Traveller* gathered headway. By now we were nearer the Oisgheir Rock than any other land and we decided to tow him there and beach him, for without a winch we could never get a living shark hove tight enough alongside the boat to take his liver out.

Oisgheir's only inhabitants are three lighthouse-keepers, to whom our arrival offered a break in the monotonous routine, as well as a means of getting off mail. Seeing us coming so slowly and listed with the weight of the shark, they could not understand what we were up to and thought there was something radically wrong with us. They were waiting at the jetty with a head-rope and a stern-rope already fast ashore, two of them leaping aboard with the ropes as we drew abreast of the jetty. It was only then that they realized that it was a shark we were towing, or that there was anyone in the area fishing for them. The length of the shark, which was only four feet less than the boat, surprised them, for had they not actually seen it they would not have believed that a boat of her size could handle such a fish.

We could not allow the keepers to tie their ropes, for the minute we eased the engine, the shark, finding himself with rope to play with, started his antics all over again, and this would never do alongside a jetty. When we explained that we wanted to beach the shark, they suggested that we should do so below the light. The third keeper ran round to a point on the shore where he indicated that we should come in. As we ran in, the shark grounded first and we were therefore able to keep him there while the man ashore made the harpoon rope fast to a convenient rock. As the tide was ebbing he soon dried, enabling us to go back to the lighthouse jetty and tie up. The keepers entertained us to an excellent dinner including homegrown vegetables and fresh milk, for the Oisgheir Rock is really a small island which the keepers use to the best advantage. They have a wonderful garden and keep a pair of goats and numerous hens. We were to learn that the keepers have an excellent workshop, which I suppose is very necessary when they are cut off for long periods in winter time. They even had a piece of belt, which they not only gave us but fitted for us in their workshop. They helped us to remove eighteen hundredweights of liver from the shark. One of them cut a huge piece of skin, almost the entire belly which was mottled white and blue, with which he hoped to cover the back of a chair, and pictures of them standing on the back of the shark were taken for their families to see. With the liver in barrels in the hold, and their letters to be posted in Mallaig, we left at high tide, towing the carcase behind, which we dumped in deep water a couple of miles out.

We saw no more sharks until the following evening when a pair of ring-net boats, working off the western end of Canna, signalled to us. A man standing in the point of a herring-boat's stem, waving an oilskin, is the recognized signal to come along-side. On getting up to them I recognized the *Kittiwake* and the *Kestrel*, both from Campbeltown, and away inshore from them several large, black dorsal fins, the reason for their signals. We made full speed for the sharks, selected our fish and soon had a harpoon fast. The shark towed us out at a fair speed and as we passed the herring-boats I shouted my thanks. As soon as the shark slowed down, we set about towing him and, by the time we were winching him up, the herring-boats had finished hauling in their nets and had come out to watch the sport. Thank God they did! The shark broke surface like a porpoise and belly-flopped not more than six feet from the boat, sending sheets of water into the air, and began at once to batter us to bits with his tail. Thinking that the fish had too much slack to play with, I heaved on the winch for all I was worth without gaining a single inch and expecting every minute that the rope would break.

'Heave in the slack, for God's sake, before he breaks up the boat!' Johnny shouted, for he could see plenty of slack harpoon wire every time the shark reared out of the water.

'I can't,' I shouted back, 'see what the hell's wrong with the roller in the stem. It's bar tight to there.'

A glance and he could see for himself, so, dodging the tail as only he could, he jumped over the rope to look over the port side of the stem.

'Hell's bells, Tex,' he roared, 'the blighter's got the harpoon wire in below the stem iron and can neither get up nor down!'

The cage roller, through which the harpoon rope was led, was to port of the stem and the shark, by surfacing on the starboard side, had passed the harpoon wire below the keel, where it had caught in the gap where the stem and keel irons just failed to meet. In one of his forward lunges he had torn this half-inch-thick strip of steel away from the stem, and I, by heaving on the winch, had jammed the wire 'good and proper'.

It quickly became obvious to the ring-net men that there was something wrong, but it was only when we set the engine off full speed astern to help the shark pull the stem iron out of the boat that they realized that we were trying to get away from him. I found myself regretting that the *Traveller* was so strong, for the iron held firm, despite the shark's mighty jerks. One of the herring-boats came closer and, cupping my hands, I bellowed an explanation above the noise of the engine.

'We'll give you a pluck, Tex,' they shouted back. 'And maybe together we'll pull the stem iron out of her.'

They circled round and flung a rope across. When we had it fast at the stern samson post there began the strangest tug-o'-war I've ever heard of. A big basking shark versus a 34-foot sharker going astern, and a fifty-foot herring-boat going ahead, with the *Traveller's* stem iron as the prize. As the huge nails pulled out one by one and the stem iron straightened out towards the shark we could see that the shackle on the harpoon wire was by now a couple of feet up the stem iron. The tremendous strain that was suddenly transferred to the harpoon rope was too much for it and it parted at once, snapping like so much string. The shark had won, and with one last derisive splash of his tail he disappeared, together with the harpoon, wire, stem iron and all. Fortunately for us our misadventures did not run in threes and the rest of the week passed without mishap, although we spent the remainder of that season with an unprotected stem.

That weekend we heard in Mallaig that we were not going to have the Minch to ourselves. Harry Thompson and George Langford had gone into partnership with a Mr. O'Connor. The idea that George and Harry were coming back was not displeasing, for it is always a comforting thought to know that there is another boat fishing the same grounds. As far as I can remember, it was during the first few weeks of May that they put in an appearance.

Chapter Five

That season ended almost in disaster and had we not been so near land at the time we would surely have lost the boat. I had found that, as the season advances, the sharks move north and that many of the shoals contain only small fish, which are not encountered at all during the first part of the season. One morning we had come upon a great pack of small sharks in Loch Rodel in Harris and were catching them three a penny, but what they lacked in size they made up in agility, several of them leaping clean out of the water on being harpooned. The weather was not very good and even in the shelter of the loch there was an annoying hash of short, steep seas. Because of this the sharks were showing on the surface only at the crest of a wave, the next moment they would go down as it broke over them. We found it difficult to get into position for a shot and rammed a good number of them in doing this. We were afraid that, should we ram too many of them, we might scare the entire pack out of the loch into the open Minch. We were up at the head of the loch, stalking a particularly large fish, when all the sharks submerged simultaneously, as if by some prearranged signal. This is a thing I have often seen but can find no explanation for. We felt sure the sharks were off but eased the engine down to dead slow with only enough way to keep her head slowly lifting and falling with each successive wave in case they should re-surface. Without any warning Johnny jerked the gun to maximum depression and pulled the trigger. I was not prepared for this for I had seen no shark; actually I was out of the wheelhouse, steering the boat with my feet, and had to dive inside to reach the gear

Johnny McInerney in action at the Traveller's *gun. Note the large coil of rope aft of the mast. Several fathoms of this rope are also coiled below the muzzle, the object being to give Johnny time to get out of the way before the main coil starts going out.*

Close-up of the Norwegian sharker Barmoy's *gun, which is typical of the guns used by the Norwegians.*

Myself loading Maxwell's gun aboard the Sea Leopard. *This is before Martini actions were fitted to the guns. The handlebar grips were for Maxwell: I personally did not like them as I found it virtually impossible to get a good grip of the gun in bad weather without firing it, because the trigger was operated by the erstwhile 'brakes'. My beard came later, after I had burned my face with one of my own guns.*

One of my earliest sharks, from the days of Maxwell's hand harpoons, being hauled up on the slip in Mallaig. The boy having a free ride does not come into the book.

Maxwell's Factory on Soay in working order. A large male shark is hauled up on the stance. In the foreground is a heap of the round cartaliginous vertebrae of previous catches.

One of the Shark Factory workers examines the inside of a shark's mouth. His right hand rests on the lower jaw.

Skinning a shark at the Soay Factory, with another one hauled up on the slip in the background.

Myself rowing out to the Traveller *in the coble which was used to bring ashore our furniture.*

Furniture being loaded into the big salmon coble in Sandy's Port at the evacuation. Behind the steamer, Hebrides, *can be seen the Skye shore.*

My wife and I.

My wife and our son, Duncan, feeding the hens.

The house on Soay. The small building in lower centre of the picture is the goat-shed.

Myself and Duncan, then aged 3½.

lever in order to check our forward way and I therefore missed seeing the shark when it almost stood on its head, as Johnny later explained to me, and came crashing down to hit the boat just aft of the wheelhouse. Nevertheless I got the full benefit of the accompanying shower of spray which completely enveloped the wheelhouse and soaked me to the skin. The suddenness of this unexpected and unwelcome soaking hindered me, and before I was able to get her out of gear Johnny was down by the wheel-house shouting: 'You all right, Tex?'

The amount of water the shark flung aboard had made it impossible for him to see where the tail had actually landed. Shaking myself like a wet spaniel I replied: 'I'm OK, but what the hell did you fire at?'

Before he could reply there was a succession of sickening bangs on the rudder and the tiller began to career from side to side, striking the towing posts at the end of each swing until one extra big wallop broke it in half and sent it spinning away over the side. Johnny told me that a shark had surfaced just ahead of us on the top of an oncoming wave, swimming straight for us with its mouth wide open. As the fish slid down into the trough it was so close to the harpoon when he depressed the gun that he could not resist the temptation to pull the trigger and see if the shark could swallow it, but for this bit of fun we were to pay dearly. I could not come out of the wheelhouse the usual way but had to climb down into the engine room and come on deck through the hatch in case the shark should knock me over the side with what remained of the wildly flailing tiller.

I jumped down and hearing the noise of running water behind me was horrified to see that water was pouring in, between the stern-tube and the stern-post. When I touched the tube I found it to be quite loose. Pushing it back into position decreased the intake a little but did not stop it; there was still enough water coming in to sink us in a very short time. When I did not appear on deck at once, Johnny came to the engine room hatch and, seeing the water pouring in, ran to the bilge pump and started pumping away for dear life, leaving the shark still battering away at the after end of the boat.

There was very little I could do to stop the flow of water, so I leapt up on deck, meaning to cut the shark away before he put the boat in bits. It was only then that the horrible truth dawned on me, the shark had somehow got the harpoon rope fast in the propeller and with all his leaping about it was impossible for me to lean over the side to cut the rope between him and the propeller. With our long-handled knife this would have been easy had the shark been dead or even quiescent, but now he would have to be killed, and quickly.

As he reared out of the water I inflicted some terrible wounds with the twenty-six-inch blade, but as the brain is about six inches back from the point of the nose and only the size of a sixpence I could not get at it. In an effort to sever the spinal cord I unfortunately got my unwieldy weapon embedded too firmly in the vertebra and he pulled it out of my hands, only to bring it crashing back on to the rail, where the handle broke like a carrot. This time the shark dived deeper and whatever part of the rope had been round the propeller suddenly cleared. Johnny, until now still pumping away and taking no part in the fight other than shouting encouragement to me and showering curses on the shark, caught up the harpoon rope and made it fast to the forward towing post. I contemplated cutting the shark away at once but as he was towing us shorewards I decided to let him carry on until he altered course. I explained to Johnny as best I could what was going on below and, leaving him once more at the pump, I jumped back down again, hammered a couple of nails into the ribs close to the tube, which I pushed back into position and secured to the nails, and tied a piece of rag round the lot, which reduced the flow to a mere trickle.

The whole operation took only a very few minutes and when I came on deck I found that we were not moving at all; the shark had stopped towing, and the rope was leading straight down. Johnny and I took turns at the pump and it was not long before

we had emptied the bilges. As we did not want to disturb the propeller shaft, we hauled him back at once with the winch. We
found this fairly easy, for a fish hooked in the mouth does not have
the same freedom of movement as one with the line in the middle
of his body, and it was only minutes before we had him up to the
stem; then, passing the lasso round the harpoon rope, we slid it
over his head and we had him. The moment we put the boat in
gear there was a fearful clatter from the engine room. This time
the stern tube had come right out of her stern and was no longer
acting as a bearing for the propeller shaft and of course the volume
of water pouring in was much worse than before. I knocked the
engine out of gear and forced the tube back into position, shouting to Johnny to pump away or we would go to the bottom. This
time I managed to secure the stern-gland with the aid of a couple
of six-inch nails hammered into the stern-post before coming on
deck. I suggested we should try to get to the pier at Rodel Hotel,
or, if the boat should fill before we reached it, run her up on the
beach.

'Set her away then,' Johnny shouted, 'before the shark comes
aboard!'

It had renewed its efforts to smash in our side with frantic tail-
lashing and so away we went full speed for the pier. Luckily it was
high water and if the boat would float long enough we could get
into the basin below the hotel. The boat was very hard to steer
with only a stump of a tiller so I lashed a boat-hook to it. Despite
Johnny's efforts the water-level rose rapidly so I put the tiller in a
central position and went down to see how the stern tube was
holding. It was still in place but had slackened, and this forced me
to take the engine out of gear and calk between the stern-gland
and the stern-post with more rags. I did not get time to make as
good a job as I would have liked, for at that juncture Johnny yelled
to me: 'Come to hell out of there and steer the boat or we'll be
ashore!'

The moment I straightened her out I relieved him at the pump.
The shark, only a little fellow in the first place and with his head

hove out of the water, did not hinder us very much, so we decided that as he had caused us so much trouble we would stick to him to the bitter end. We had only a couple of hundred yards to go at the most, although the concentrated effort we put into our spells of pumping made it seem much farther, more especially so as the water-level continued to rise. On reaching the basin we kept the boat going all out, with the water now well up to the engine and the flywheel throwing it about like sparks from a catherine wheel. We managed to get alongside the quay before the water drowned the magneto, stopping the engine dead. I jumped ashore and hauled the boat as far as she would float, grounding her about 100 yards from the hotel. We paid no attention to the excited guests who came running down the quay on seeing the strange boat with what to them must have appeared a huge fish alongside, asking all the usual questions, what is it? where did you get it? and so on. We were too busy getting the shark clear of the boat.

When the tide receded the guests were able to examine the fish for themselves and we were able to see the extent of the damage. We found that the propeller shaft was bent and that the outside gland on the stern-tube was almost screwed off. We had to un-couple the shaft and draw it out; then, removing the propeller, we straightened out the shaft as best we could with a sledge-hammer. On reassembling the stern-gear, when screwing back the outside gland into the stern-tube, we found that the screws which held it in place were sheered off flush with the stern-post. We had to insert a leather washer between the post and the gland so that when it was screwed up flush there was wood behind the scre-wholes instead of the stumps of the screws. The following morning brought a full gale which blew constantly for several days and when at last it blew itself out we started her up and set off on our ninety-mile journey home – towing the carcase, minus its liver, much to the relief of the hotelier.

The shaft was not any too straight and by the time we had dumped the shark in deep water the stern-tube began to leak again, but this was maybe all for the best for the constant trickle of cold water probably kept the shaft from heating too quickly. I cannot now remember how far across the Minch we were when the shaft became so hot that we were obliged to take the engine out of gear and let it cool, but I do remember that we had to do this very often until we were about halfway across the Minch, when it began to blow quite hard from the north-west. On hoisting our sail we were soon scudding along before the wind. By the time we reached Neist Point the wind had increased and as the tide was with us we did not use the engine until we reached An Dubh Sgeir, a particularly nasty chain of reefs that jut out almost a mile from the shore. We maintained this starting and stopping business as the shaft grew too hot all the way to Mallaig. We did not get much rest from the pump on our journey home but all went well and we came steaming into Mallaig harbour late that evening with twenty-five barrels of liver, as if nothing out of the ordinary had happened.

Early next morning, as the liver was somewhat older than usual, we were abroad bright and early in order to get the barrels away on the early train. Later on when Johnny and I were washing down the boat at the pier, the village constable came down and began to pass the time of day. We had not been chatting long when he slipped in a question: 'When were you last in Rum?'

I knew at once what he was getting at and so did Johnny and we determined to get a rise out of him.

'Rum?' we said. 'We were there last week.' Thus encouraged, he asked us what we were doing ashore, to which we countered: 'What would we be doing ashore?'

In actual fact as we were going into Rum we had seen a boat very similar to the *Traveller* coming out. It took some time to get the constable to own up to an interest in deer and then it transpired that the gamekeepers on Rum had surprised a couple of men poaching deer; they had managed to escape and had made off in the general direction of Mallaig. I got the impression that he was convinced it had been us, so I rather took the wind out of his sails when I told him that when we wanted a deer on Rum we had no need to go ashore – all we had to do was to fit a light line to a small harpoon and cruise along the shore until we spotted a likely beast, harpoon him and haul him aboard ... His face was a study, and with a final snort of disgust he turned on his heel and stalked up the pier.

He had obviously heard, at fourth or fifth hand, the story of a run-in I had had some years previously with a certain Highland proprietor. As the story had obviously grown in the telling the original version might be of interest.

I am far too fond of deer-stalking, let alone the deer themselves, to go poaching for them, and anyway I have a great many friends, deer-stalkers on the surrounding estates, part of whose duties it is to keep the deer-poachers off the mountains. Salmon were quite another matter, and one which I considered came under the heading of good clean sport. I have never heard of any salmon-poacher in this district using any device more deadly than a small splash net. The commercial poacher using explosives or any of his obnoxious poisons would not last long hereabouts; every man's hand, including those of the local poachers, would be against him. There is no doubt that without a certain amount of help and 'watching-the-wall-while-the-gentlemen-go-by' most poachers would never stand a chance.

I had myself occasionally enjoyed the thrill of poaching – but there was one particularly attractive river, vigilantly watched, which I had never attempted to poach.

One day, over a dram, I learned that the watcher's cottage was empty and that there was a sporting chance that the river would be unwatched for a day or two. Here was an opportunity too good to miss, a chance to poach salmon from the river, in daylight and without being disturbed.

As there appeared to be small risk of being caught if everything worked out according to plan, two friends of mine seized the chance of coming with me. It was a carefully planned enterprise.

We set off in my little motor-launch, ostensibly to go mackerel-fishing; an evening's mackerel-fishing was no unusual thing for anybody. We therefore felt sure that no one would think twice about where we were going, unless they registered the fact that we were towing a dinghy. Even so, the presence of the dinghy was offset by that of my two respectable friends, who surely would take no part in any reprehensible escapades. We fished for mackerel for a couple of hours and filled a few boxes. Any salmon we caught later could be smuggled ashore quite openly by laying them in the bottom of a fish-box and covering them over with mackerel.

The cottage vacated by the retiring gamekeeper was one of the most isolated in the area, its nearest neighbour being over a dozen miles away. It was our plan of campaign to arrive at the coveted river about low water, run the launch as far into the estuary as she would float, and get ashore somewhere in the dinghy, which we would then haul up the beach above high-water mark. I cannot now remember why we had not taken my own small dinghy, which could be carried aboard the launch, but had instead decided to tow the larger, more cumbersome boat belonging to one of my partners in crime. On arrival at the river mouth we altered our plans slightly and anchored the launch in deep water, some hundred yards off the shore, in among some small wooded islands, where she would be reasonably well hidden, and we all three climbed into the dinghy. On reaching the shore it did not take us long to realize that it was impossible for us to drag the dinghy over the sand to above high-water mark where she would be within reach when the tide came in. It was decided that one of us must row back to the launch and wait until the tide made sufficiently to get into the river with the dinghy. The other two would stay ashore and set off up river about three-quarters of a mile to the highest pool, and start netting the pools on the way back to the river mouth. As none of us wanted to miss any of the sport, three straws were produced and I, drawing the short one, was left to look after the dinghy. Cursing my luck I rowed back to the launch and brewed myself a cup of tea. To while away the time I topped up the fuel tanks from some spare five-gallon tins I carried aboard, filled up the little petrol squirt used for starting the engine and put all in order for getting under way quickly on our return.

I managed to get the dinghy ashore at the mouth of the river where some alder scrub grew almost to the water's edge, at least three hours before high water. I had hardly tied the painter when, from away up the mountainside, three shots rang out in rapid succession, re-echoing again and again through the high tops. Here at the lochside I could see nothing above me because of the alder thicket and was thankful that I had such excellent cover. Emerging on the other side of the thicket I lay down among the bracken and waited for some movement of either deer or men to indicate the position of whoever had fired the shots. I must have lain there for half an hour before I saw anything move, when on the skyline high above me a man on horseback appeared. He was followed by a cavalcade of men and horses. There were at least fifteen men and four or five horses. Slipping back into the thicket I pulled the boat further in on the rising tide and covered her with branches and bracken, camouflaging her as best I could. When I thought the boat was well hidden, I crept out again to lie and watch what was to happen next. The cavalcade continued down the hill, straight for where I lay, but seemed to be in no hurry, which made me feel certain that they had spotted neither me nor the boat.

As they drew nearer, I guessed that the man on horseback was the proprietor accompanied by his head stalker, and other estate workers pressed into service as ghillies or ponymen. Three of the ponies were carrying stags. I had not bargained for this and was desperately anxious about the safety of my two friends, whom I had talked into coming with me. By now they would be working their way down the river and might even be coming into view of the stalking party.

Eventually the party came down to the riverside and swung right along the path, passing some twenty yards from where I lay. I watched them all go on towards the empty gamekeeper's cottage, where they stopped and took the deer off the pack ponies. The proprietor disappeared into the cottage and the remainder prepared to have their lunch.

Chapter Five

I lay watching until they had finished, wondering what on earth I was to do about it, and where they intended to go. Their intentions soon became obvious when the proprietor came out, mounted his pony, and started to lead the party up the riverside away from me but straight in the direction from which I expected my companions to appear. This would never do. They must not be caught red-handed poaching with my net and, if they had had any luck at all, a salmon or two into the bargain. The stalking party must be side-tracked, and I must act as decoy.

There was an old Army gas-cape lying in the dinghy so I slipped back and got it, stuffed it with bracken, and with some string quickly fashioned it into the form of a rucksack which I tied in place on my back. I hoped that from a distance I would pass as that curse of all deer-stalkers, the unauthorized mountain climber, although I was clad in only a singlet, grey flannels and a pair of canvas sneakers. Slipping quietly into the river, I made my way upstream as quickly as possible. The steep banks on either side hid me from view and I was not quite up abreast of the rearguard when I found I could go no further without coming into sight. I quickly swam across, emerging among some huge boulders on the other side, and set off for the roughest route I could see up the mountain, as if I hadn't a care in the world. Completely ignoring the shooting party on the other side of the river, I reached the first of the rocks at the foot of the mountain before I was spotted. Climbing on to a boulder I turned and waved to them as if I had only just seen them. The proprietor stopped dead and I saw the flash of his telescope as he drew it from its case. Next minute he shouted: 'Come back, you there! Where do you think you're going?'

My only answer was to wave again, pretending that I had not heard; then, turning my back on them, I started to climb. This action justifiably annoyed the gentleman on the other side of the river and he immediately spurred his pony and splashed into the river after me, but I had chosen my place well and before he emerged on my side I was well above him and keeping always to the rocks. He galloped about this way and that, trying to find a way up for his horse, but every time the rocks beat him, while I climbed steadily on. His men crossed, fanned out, and began to come after me. I had no worry that they would catch me, but I had to lose them somehow in order to warn my friends.

Eventually I crossed the shoulder of the mountain and started down the other side as fast as I could go, running whenever possible. Nevertheless it seemed ages before I got down to the river again, for I had been climbing away from the river, seawards, when in view of the stalkers. I was pretty exhausted when I met my friends and hardly waited for explanations but cleared off up the hill on the other side of the river, where all three of us lay down in a clump of bracken for a council of war.

We discussed and rejected several plans for getting out of the glen and down to the boat. I was insistent that so long as the shooting party thought that I was alone there was no sense in letting them know otherwise. We decided that I should go alone down the river and try to get to the dinghy and, if I was spotted and chased, try to get aboard and make off. I could then return after dark for my two friends. They were to follow me at a respectable distance and not to move when they could not see me. If I was spotted before I got to the dinghy, I would lead them away from the boat, leaving my companions a clear field to get to the dinghy themselves and make off. The net I stuffed into the gascape in place of the bracken and, carrying two large salmon tied by their tails round my waist, away I went downstream, sometimes swimming, sometimes wading.

All went well and I saw no sign of the shooting party until the gamekeeper's cottage came in sight. There I could see the ponies grazing in the walled paddock below it. So I lay down out of sight of it and signalled to my companions to come on. We waited there until we were certain that most if not all of the shooting party were in or around it, for I counted nine men outside. Soon most of the men went into the cottage, where no doubt someone had made tea. Once again I entered the river, leaving my friends to follow on after me if I was not spotted. There was a great deal of bracken there which afforded me excellent cover and I made good progress. A couple of hundred yards from the cottage the cover gave out. Even worse, the river widened and its banks were less steep. Here I was forced to crawl forward on my hands and knees, with little more than my head above water.

At last I got abreast of the cottage where the wall round the paddock would hide me for most of the way to the thicket where I had left the dinghy. Sliding on my belly like a seal, I crept out of the water, praying that no one would come and look over the wall. Having gained the shelter of the wall without mishap, I found an old overgrown ditch running parallel with it deep enough for me to get into. In I went and lay panting for a moment or two, regaining my breath before darting for the dinghy. I felt I had pushed my luck far enough.

Then, without further ado, I scurried to the corner of the wall and stopped for a last look round before making my final dash for the dinghy. I had no means of knowing where the proprietor had posted his men, but no one was in sight. So, clutching my two salmon like a woman her skirts, I sprinted as I had never sprinted before, gained the thicket and got into the dinghy. I had no idea whether I had been seen or not, nor of the whereabouts of my two companions.

I pushed the boat quietly into the river and started rowing upstream. I did not have to go far before I could see my companions crouching by the same boulders where I had crossed the river earlier in the day. They must have been in good heart, for one of them was waving a large salmon to attract my attention. I was soon up to them and had them aboard, complete with the rest of their catch which they had so stoically retained all the way down stream. Rowing for all I was worth, and greatly helped by the current, we were soon out and alongside the launch. Springing aboard I made for the engine and started it at once, while my companions hauled up the anchor and we were under way.

It was not until we were clear of the islands that we were seen by the stalkers, who came running down the beach shouting and waving their arms. Surely they did not expect us to turn back. Easing down the engine I passed them 100 yards off-shore and waved to them but made no remark. My two companions the while had remained hidden in the fo'c'sle, for they had not been seen by anyone at all, and there was no sense in getting their names coupled with mine in poaching activities. With a final wave I put the little engine into full speed and set off for home.

It was only then that I realized the significance of the shouting and signalling. It was not me that it was intended for, but a large and fast motor yacht which came steaming into view round the end of the islands. We made straight for her and I shouted a greeting to her surprised skipper.

In a few moments we had turned a bend and were out of sight. My companions emerged with a mug of tea and some sandwiches for me. I suggested that they go back where they came from before the yacht had time to make after me, and sat back at the tiller to enjoy my tea and await developments. I was not left waiting long, for I was still drinking my tea when the yacht came round the headland, steaming all out and bearing down on us so fast that I felt they might run us down. I pretended to be oblivious of her progress in our direction. It was only when she came up alongside with a great swirl of foam at her stern as her engines were put into reverse that I let them see that I was aware of them.

The two boats came together and I shouted up to the skipper to be careful. My words, however, were drowned by the voice of the proprietor calling to his skipper to close with us as he wished to board my boat and search it. This I forestalled by knocking my engine out of gear, and slipping round the yacht's stern, I stood off on his other side.

The yacht circled round and came up alongside again, and one of the crew lowered a fender, but I kept going full speed, making it difficult for the yacht's skipper to hold his there without pushing me ashore.

'What the hell are you up to?' I roared with assumed anger to the skipper as I put my engine into full speed astern, and the two boats fell away.

As I did this my two companions popped their heads out of the fo'c'sle door with gleeful grins on both their faces. 'Well done, Tex! Keep him out of here for the love of Mike. If he sees the fish we are done for!'

As the yacht was now coming up fast behind us, they popped back in and slid the door across. I kept my little boat going all out and the moment the yacht's engines were eased I went full speed astern again. The yacht, being heavier, carried her way longer, and we again slipped astern.

After several unsuccessful attempts to get alongside without ramming me, the yacht changed her tactics. She came slowly up parallel with me, a boat's length off. Her owner came to the rail and, cupping his hands, shouted: 'Don't think you have escaped. I'll be home in plenty of time to phone the police, who will intercept you on the pier-head.'

With that he signalled to the wheelhouse and away the yacht went full out, leaving a great wake of white foam behind her, and me to plod along home to meet my Waterloo when I got there.

Soon the yacht was out of sight round a turn of the loch and my two companions came aft to join me at the tiller.

'What now, Tex?' they asked. 'We are sure to get caught if we try to get the salmon ashore when we get home.'

'Why go home?' I countered. 'You fellows can go, but I'm certainly not going to give up the salmon now, nor am I going to throw them overboard. It will be almost dark when we get in and I can land you chaps with the dinghy before we get to the harbour. Let's carry on anyway and see what happens.'

By the time we were up abreast of the harbour, it had started to rain and blow quite hard from the south and west. As darkness fell the wind grew and soon we were battling half a gale. This was a blessing in disguise for it made the night as black as pitch and we felt quite safe in slipping round to the back of the harbour. I went ashore with the dinghy leaving my two companions to look after the launch. Here on a rocky promontory are crammed a weird and wonderful assortment of wooden huts in varying states of repair, most of which house the fisher-lassies who follow the herring fleet from one end of the country to the other. I made straight for the nearest 'girls' dormitory', where I safely concealed both nets and salmon.

In a matter of minutes I was back aboard the launch and steaming for the lights of the harbour. There was nothing to fear from anyone now, for there were no tell-tale salmon scales aboard the boat – the scales of a salmon are much larger than mackerel scales. We had hidden the salmon, when we were up the loch, by burying them in the boxes of mackerel, and had put them in sacks before putting them ashore. My two companions had gone off before the police officers arrived. They made a thorough search of the launch, but they could not prove what I had been up to, though I dare say they suspected a lot.

Chapter Six

The sharkfishing season is naturally a short one, and Johnny and I had intended to follow it with lobster-fishing, but the sharks had made such a mess of the boat, quite apart from the damage to the stern-gear, that she would need an extensive overhaul before she was fit for the winter seas. We therefore both decided to go our own ways until the following March, when we would once again put the boat in order for the sharks.

We slipped the *Traveller* for the winter and Johnny went off deerstalking, which was his normal practice at this time of year. I myself went back to sea for the winter as engineer in one of the local ring-net boats.

The ring-net is a comparatively new method of fishing for herring and requires a pair of boats to work it, with a crew of six in each boat. The *Spindrift*, the boat I joined, was really a lovely craft, for John Smith, her skipper and owner, keeps her like a yacht. A ring-net skipper nearly always owns his own boat and has her built to his own specifications. The *Spindrift* was built in 1946 by Jimmy Noble of Fraserburgh of the finest Scotch larch on oak frames; she is fifty-three feet eight inches long, sixteen feet nine broad, with a draught of six feet. She is powered by an eighty-eight-hp Kelvin diesel which gives her a speed of nine to ten knots and she carries fuel for seventy-five hours running at full speed. There are seven bunks in her fo'c'sle and her hold has a capacity of 170 cran of herring. She is all varnished above the waterline, including decks and spars, and every bit of ironwork about her is galvanised and frequently painted with aluminium paint. In the wheel-house is the echometer, an electrical depth recorder, and fish are marked on the paper graph as an obstruction of the echo between the boat's bottom and the sea-bed. In this way the skipper can see at a glance the extent of a shoal of herring and how far it is from the surface. There is also a wireless transmitter and receiver with which the boats can keep in touch with each other. Such a boat when new would cost about £7,000 and £50 a time to revarnish her. Each ring-net boat must have several nets and this is quite an item as they cost £520 each for the bare net without the spring-ropes, buoys, etc. These nets are usually three hundred and fifty fathoms long and twenty-five fathoms deep and it is not unusual to lose a net altogether, unable to hold it, let alone haul it back, if it has been shot in heavy weather, or in a place where the strength of the tide is such that it carries the net away in spite of us.

The ring-net fishing grounds in the winter are all along the east coast of the Outer Hebrides and as herring are always caught during the hours of darkness the skipper has to have extensive local knowledge, for which no number of charts is any substitute. There must be a colossal amount of herring caught by this method on the west coast of Scotland alone, for I have seen twenty special trains leave Mallaig in one day crammed full of herring, and have counted the lights of fifty pairs of boats in Barra Sound at the southern end of the Outer Hebrides.

Here to illustrate the method is a hypothetical case. The *Spindrift* having located a shoal of herring with the echometer at a depth within the scope of the net, signals to her neighbour boat the *Margaret Ann*, by putting on some prearranged coloured light or cluster of lights, that she is about to shot her net. If she were not to signal, the two boats might shot simultaneously, which would result in both of them having to haul their nets in again end-on, for, as I have already said, it requires two boats to work the net properly. When the *Spindrift* is certain that she is over the thickest part of the shoal, she shots away at once, casting first her spring-rope with a 'winkie' attached to the end some ten fathoms back from the net. The net proper is, of course, attached to this rope along its 'sole' or bottom. She steams full speed round in a half circle, paying out the net and spring-rope as she goes. To ensure easy shotting, the net is carefully laid-on ready as far aft as is possible on the port side and the boats are so designed that there are no obstructions. The winkie may well be described as a long three-cell waterproof torch wearing a lifebelt, with the bottom part weighted to keep its head up when floating.

As soon as the *Margaret Ann* sees the winkie in the water she makes full speed for it, picks it up, makes the rope fast, and tows the net round to meet the *Spindrift*, thus completing the ring from which the method gets its name. When the two boats meet they always come together on their starboard sides, which are completely lined with heavy motor tyres for fenders, for in bad weather they could damage each other. At this stage several things happen at once and each man has his respective station. Four of the crew of the *Margaret Ann* jump aboard the *Spindrift*, bringing the end of the spring-rope they have been towing and another rope, which we call the towing rope, together with the *Spindrift*'s winkie and the buoy which has been keeping up the rope. The *Spindrift* until now has been towing the net with a similar spring-rope and both ropes will be passed through a roller on her port side and led to the winch; then, as quickly as possible, she will begin heaving them in simultaneously, one on each winch barrel.

The towing rope will by now be fast halfway down the *Spindrift*'s starboard side and its other end attached to the *Margaret Ann* by the remaining member of her crew and she will have started to tow the *Spindrift* gently by the broadside. Unless this is done the *Spindrift* would quickly winch herself right into the middle of her own net. When the net is reached, it is heaved in by hand, eight men spacing themselves from stem to stern on her port side. The remaining two, the skipper and the engineer, continue winching in the spring-rope. This greatly assists the men at the net for the spring-rope is fastened to the bottom of the net by rope stoppers at two-fathom intervals. These stoppers can be cast off the spring as they come to the rollers and the bottom of the net can be hauled aboard separately. All this is done as quickly as possible in order to make a bag out of which there is no escape for the fish. The net is hauled actually from the bottom until all the herring are herded together as tightly as possible. The centre part of the net, which we call the bag, is made of heavier twine and has more corks at the top and five large inflatable buoys to ensure that it does not go down with the weight of the catch. If there is herring in the net the two men left aboard the *Margaret Ann* will have prepared their hold to receive them, made ready their derrick and rigged their brailer with which to lift them aboard. When all is ready the towing rope is cast off and the *Margaret Ann* will steam round and station herself parallel with the *Spindrift*, port-side to port-side, with the bag of herring between the two boats. She then catches up one of the buoys attached to the net, hauls it aboard and removes it before making the net fast to her rail; perhaps I should add that the port sides of both boats are completely devoid of fenders.

With the net strapped along her side she will make herself fast fore and aft to the *Spindrift*, but with slack ropes. At this juncture the two cooks, whose job it is, will station themselves fore and aft on the *Spindrift* and keep the two boats about ten feet apart with the aid of long poles. The *Margaret Ann*'s engineer will take his station at his own winch to haul up his brailer. I have already described a brailer; the only difference between this one and mine is a light line fast to the peak of the foolscap, and this line is passed aboard the other boat to stretch the net out before filling it with herring. Another line is attached to a bridle on the hoop and with this rope the brailer is hauled through the herring to fill it; the man who wields the brailer pole can do little other than guide it and Heaven help him should he let it go through the bottom of the net and let the herring escape. This job is invariably done by the skipper and calls for more skill than might be imagined. About three cran is lifted at a time and quickly disappears down a couple of manhole hatches in the sidedeck into the hold where, being alive, the herring soon level themselves off. Herring coming up alive in the net often squeak, just like mice, when touched.

The hold is arranged in sections which are removable board by board and to trim the boat it may be necessary to remove some of them to allow the herring into these sections. The object of these section boards is to keep the herring stable when the boat is rolling in bad weather, for they may rub the skin, and even their tails, off themselves. If this happens we refer to them as 'washed' herring and there is no hope of selling them for human consumption.

When the last herring is brailed aboard, the *Margaret Ann's* crew clear out at once, back to their own boat to continue to look for herring, while the *Spindrift's* crew, with all their working lights blazing, carefully lay on their net again, ready for shotting, that is with the exception of the skipper who must steer the boat, following his neighbour.

I have a special regard for the *Spindrift*, and was among the few on John's side when she came in for the usual criticism the day she arrived new in Mallaig, for John had departed slightly from the ordinary. He had had her made finer forward than was usual, to give her greater speed, and the pierhead critics predicted that with a full load she would be down by the head. They were wrong, for she can carry much more herring than even John had anticipated. Although she is fine in the head, the critics had forgotten to look at her shoulders, the width of which would keep her up, and still she is faster than any of her neighbours. That, however, is not the only reason I have a regard for her, for in all probability she saved my life and those of the entire crew of the *Margaret Ann*.

One winter season I was at sea in the *Margaret Ann*, seine-net fishing, which unlike the ring-net does not necessitate a neighbour. Returning from the fishing grounds off the island of Coll on a particularly dark and stormy night, we were making all speed for the shelter of Aringour harbour. We were just abreast of the rocks known as the Cairns of Coll when, without the slightest warning, our engine stopped dead. On lifting the engine-room hatch to go down to investigate I was enveloped in a cloud of smoke the smell of which I recognized to be burning paint. We found that the engine had seized up because a piece of seaweed had choked our seacock, depriving the engine of water for the cooling system. We were so close to the rocks that it was useless to drop an anchor, and the strength of wind was such that it would not be many minutes before we would be blown ashore. I vividly remember offering Jim Manson the skipper an inflatable lifejacket I used as a pillow, for he, as is common among fishermen, cannot swim.

'Fire that damn thing over the side!' he had said. 'If I'm going to drown, I'll do it quick. To hell with hanging about freezing all night!'

Nothing I could do would make him put it on. We were all grouped round the wheelhouse waiting for the boat to strike the first of the rocks before making over the side, when out of nowhere, or so it seemed at the time, came the *Spindrift*, sweeping in along-side with just enough time to throw us a rope; seconds more would have been too late. We knew that she was fishing in the vicinity but had not realized that she was near enough to be able to help us. She had been coming in behind us and John Smith had noticed by our sailing lights that we had stopped; when he saw all our deck lights go on, he had assumed the worst. He opened his engine full out, giving her all she had got, and plucked us out of it in the nick of time. He towed us right into the shelter of Coll harbour. This hap-pened in the early months of 1947, which was before any of the local fishing boats were fitted with wireless, not that wireless would have been much use to us that night.

Ring-net men in the course of their work in Hebridean waters at all seasons of the year have a better opportunity than many natu-ralists for studying the habits and migrations of seals, birds and, of course, fish. For many of them their interest in and knowledge of, these creatures are both constant and surprisingly extensive. I myself have twice had in my hands, under widely differing circum-stances, one of the more rare and lesser-known birds of the northern hemisphere – Leach's forktailed petrel. The first time was on the shore between Mallaig and Morar in broad daylight. I have since learned that it is unusual to find them on land unless during the breeding season, and only then down their burrows during daylight, incubating the single egg which is characteristic of petrels. On an autumn afternoon in 1948 I met this little bird crouching on the rocks by the shore as if it was injured. It was not in the least afraid when I picked it up and it made no effort to fly away when I opened my hand to release it. There appeared to be nothing wrong with it, so I laid it down again where I had found it and it scuttled away to the darkest corner it could find among the rocks. I had never seen its like before but took it to be one of the petrel family. My description was probably inaccurate because I could never get anyone to tell me what it was, until some years later I acquired some books on bird recognition.

The second time was in September '51 when fishing with the *Spindrift* off the west coast of Ross-shire. One dirty night we came into Gairloch to shelter, in the hope that the night would yet better enough to allow us to fish. We did not go to the pier but anchored in the shelter of Longa Island. The crew had gone below with the exception of John Smith and me, who were working on the net with all the deck lights blazing when to our utter amazement a Leach's petrel landed in the net about a foot from my hand. John and I did not move for a moment or two as we did not want to scare it away, more especially so as he had never seen the bird before. This bird, like the other, made no effort to fly away; it just sat there on its haunches as if its legs were unable to keep it up. I bent forward, picked it up and examined it thoroughly, and still it showed no desire to leave its human company.

The working lights of a ringer have large shades for reflecting the light down on to the deck. Thinking that the lights were dazzling it, John tossed it into the air, whence it immediately returned, only this time it landed on the foredeck and it was still there when we went below. The weather did not allow us to go out to fish that night but the bird was gone in the morning.

Since I married I have built up a fairly good small reference library including several of the New Naturalist series, in one of which I found an article by Robert Atkinson on Leach's fork-tailed petrel, so this time I knew my bird. It has always irked me that I forgot to mention these encounters to Atkinson on the occasion when his boat and the *Traveller* were stormbound for a few days in Harris, for the study of these little pelagic petrels appeared to be his special interest.

Another thing I saw which amazed me, and had I not seen it for myself I do not believe I would have credited it, was the shepherding of a couple of hundred cran of herring several hundred yards and the driving of them right into the middle of our neighbour's net. This happened in 1947, which was before the advent of echometers in the local ring-net fleet. At that time there were three ways of locating a shoal of herring. We could see them playing like trout, only herring do not leap so far out of the water; we could see them with the 'burning', as we called the phosphorescence of the fish themselves which we could see beneath the surface as the boat approached them; but the most successful indicator of all was the wire. This wire, rather like a thirty-fathom-long piano string with a six-pound lead weight on the end, was let down to the bottom and then towed along behind the boat just off the sea-bed. It was the engineer's job to stand aft holding it, waiting until the boat would pass over a shoal of herring the extent and density of which could be felt in the wire by the intensity of the vibrations as it passed through the shoal, striking the herring in its path. Many a freezing winter's night have I spent standing at the stern of a ringer with a wire, for I was always engineer. It was hard to keep warm, as I could only walk some three paces in any direction; nor could I wear gloves for, while the sensitivity of one's fingers is rather low when they are half frozen; with a pair of gloves on it would be almost nil, and with the crew depending on the wire to locate the herring comfort was of secondary importance. I do not mean that I had to remain there the whole night through, for the engineer is frequently relieved for tea, copious quantities of which, strong and sweet, are drunk during the night. On the night to which I refer we were fishing in the South Fords, between Benbecula and South Uist. There were two pairs of boats fishing in company and I was aboard the *Margaret Ann*.

We had located a fairly large shoal of herring and had made a ring round them but they had eluded us as we had torn the net rather badly on the bottom. As soon as we had the net aboard the crew set to mending it at once with all the lights blazing, leaving the skipper to follow the *Golden Ray*, our neighbour. We were not long working on the net when we saw the *Golden Ray's* shotting lights go on and seconds later her winkie in the water astern of her, but as the other pair of boats were nearer to her than we were we did not set off to pick it up. One of them was soon up to the winkie and towing the end round to complete the circle. As soon as we saw that things were under control we paid no further attention to them. I was working at the sole rope at the port rail and on looking over the side I could hardly believe my eyes for there, on the surface right alongside the boat, were countless thousands of herring, as closely packed as if they were in a tin. I shouted to the skipper to 'Come and look at this', indicating to him that I really meant it when I had shouted 'Solid herring', by plunging a fending-off pole in among them and tossing several into the air. Jim quickly came out of the wheelhouse and had a look, joining the rest of the crew, who by this time were lined along the port side. There appeared to be none at all on the starboard side. Jim did not stare for long but jumped back into the wheelhouse and set the boat off slowly ahead, shouting: 'Swing out the brailing lights, Tex, and see if the herring stick to us.'

These lights are fastened on the end of long horizontal poles attached to swivels on the top of the wheelhouse, and with their large reflectors they direct powerful beams into the water over the side. In a second or two I was intrigued to see that all the herring had swung round and were now pointing in the same direction as the boat was slowly moving.

'They're coming with us, Jim,' I said, as I took the wheel so that he could go and see them for himself. As soon as Jim had ascertained that the herring were still with us, he ran forward to the stem and, cupping his hands, bellowed with all the power of his lungs in his usual broad Doric: 'Dinna cam tee, Peter, we're bringin' herrin' enough as full the fower boats.'

It is common knowledge that fish are attracted by bright lights, but herding them like this I had never seen or heard of before. When I later inquired of Peter, the *Golden Ray's* skipper to whom Jim had roared not to complete the ring, he said that he thought Jim was joking for he could not understand how Jim could have herring coming with him, although he was prepared to believe that there was a shoal of herring where we were. To bring them to him was another thing. Nevertheless, that is just what we did, for Peter hesitated long enough to allow us to get close enough for Jim to explain what was happening. The herring remained with us until we passed between the two boats, when we switched off all our lights as soon as we were inside the almost completed circle of net. Seconds later the circle was complete and we slipped out over the net, using wooden poles with wooden cross-pieces at their ends to push the net down. With one pole on either side of the boat, we walked aft with them, pushing the net well down clear of the propeller. The herring had very little hope of escaping below the net, for the water was shallow enough to allow it to hang like a curtain from the surface to the bottom. We went up alongside the *Golden Ray* to help in hauling. There were so many herring in the net that we eventually lashed the *Margaret Ann* to the starboard side of the *Golden Ray* and Jim and I went aboard, too. When all the herring was aboard the boats, we had 300 cran between us, which at that time fetched £4 10s. a cran.

Esprit de corps is so strong in the ring-net fleet that one has to go to sea with them to fully appreciate it. It is not a brotherhood with any badge or set of rules; in fact I might go so far as to say that no such thing would be openly acknowledged to exist, and yet individuals, and even boats, which do not conform to this powerful code quickly fade from the scene. For instance, should one crew tear their net so badly that they would be unlikely to be able to repair it for the following night's fishing, every available man, rivals included, gathers round and works at it all day in order to have it finished in time. This often means standing on a wind-swept pier in rain or hail for hours on end, with their fingers so stiff with cold that they have to look at them to make sure they are really holding the net. When one considers that these men have had no sleep at all the night before and in all probability will get none tonight, and could but for this torn net be sleeping in a comfortable bunk, it is quite a gesture. There are many other things that one would never learn about ring-net men except by going to sea with them, for moaners and agitators are weeded out at once. There is no room for them in a ring-net boat, and I know of no quicker way to find the true character of a man than to be cooped up with him for at least a week at a time, working, eating and sleeping in the confined space of a fifty-foot fishing boat.

The small but compact quarters of a ringer's fo'c'sle induce in many ring-net men a form of claustrophobia they jokingly call the 'mare'. A ring-net boat steaming across the Minch, deep down in the water, with her hold full of herring, gets a fair buffeting in the teeth of a winter gale. There are usually at least two men on watch, one at the wheel and the other keeping his eye on the engine, and also on the herring in case they should begin to move. The remainder of the crew are all in their bunks in the fo'c'sle sleeping if they can, but at least resting.

On such a night Jim Manson and I were on watch together; there were a 126 cran aboard, just about as much as she could carry and get her hatches on. The old *Margaret Ann* was a lively wee boat and although heavily laden she behaved exceedingly well. Her decks were constantly awash as she buried her nose deep into the seas, sometimes shipping them green, only to rear up to the next sea and fling the water over the side as she ploughed her way home. Under the circumstances it was impossible to have the fo'c'sle hatch open and every time I went below to look at the herring quite a lot of water accompanied me before I was able to close it. The atmosphere in the fo'c'sle can well be imagined, for the cook had stoked up the stove before retiring and not only the top of it but most of the funnel was red-hot. We had caught the herring early in the night and reckoned to arrive in Mallaig between midnight and one o'clock. Because of this unusually early arrival (we did not generally arrive until about eight a.m., the time of the first sale) Jim had suggested that I make tea and waken the crew the moment we gained the shelter of the harbour, as some of them might want to go home.

About a quarter of an hour from Mallaig I went forward, restoked the stove, put on the kettle and lashed it there, for the boat was still plunging like a bucking broncho. As there was still too much motion at the mouth of the harbour we carried on right in, meaning to tie the boat to the fishquay before going down to make the tea and waken the crew. The instant Jim eased the engine down to dead slow we were both startled by roars of anguish from the fo'c'sle and recognised the voice of one of the crew who had been at the ring-net all his working life. The roars quickly changed to bellows of frustration: 'Stop her, Jim! Come astern, damn you, astern! Astern!! ASTERN!!!'

'Go down and see what the hell's wrong with him. I'll tie her up myself,' Jim said, for we had by now come to rest alongside the quay. He was still bellowing at Jim to come astern as I flung open the hatch and jumped below where, switching on the light, I was amazed to see the sufferer still in his bunk (a top one) pushing up the deck head with both his hands and his knees. The other three men were simply leaning out of their bunks watching him and saying and doing nothing about it.

'What's up?' I asked, going forward.

'Don't touch him, he's got the "mare",' someone hastened to warn me, but they were too late, I was up to him. The moment I touched him he swung round and hit me a terrific wallop in the chest with his foot, sending me clean over the table to land crashing against the bulkhead by the hatch. This was not my idea of fun and springing to my feet in a towering rage I jumped at him meaning to drag him out of his bunk and knock some sense into him. Jim, on his way down the hatch, was quicker and grabbed me by my oil-skins, pulled me back, and held me in a bearlike hug. Jim's raucous laughter quickly cooled my temper.

'Steady on, Tex. He disna ken he kicked ye, it's only the "mare". We all get it now and again and you'll get it too some day.'

The expression on the sufferer's face when he realized what he had done made me laugh, but he took some minutes to gather his senses and tell us the reason for his roars. He had been dreaming that we were coming into a strange harbour in the dark and that he was standing up forward on the fo'c'sle head directing Jim, who was at the wheel. When we got right into this harbour he saw a huge wooden pier without a single boat tied to it; at this juncture, instead of easing the engine to dead slow, Jim had opened it up full speed and charged at the pier, which had suddenly risen up to allow the boat to pass underneath it. We got ourselves completely lost in a forest of piles, but he could see a clear way out directly astern but no one would believe him. It was only then that he began to realize that the pier above him was slowly descending to its original height, forcing him first to his knees and eventually on to his back. He was still dreaming that he was pushing up the pier in an effort to avoid being squashed when I had gone to waken him, only to be rewarded with a kick for my pains.

Since that night I have had many experiences of men with the 'mare' although I have never experienced it first-hand, and I learned to ignore them and laugh with them when they later told their weird dreams.

Somnambulation is happily almost unknown, but I do know of one case where a man was in the habit of getting out of his bunk and making for the fo'c'sle hatch. He was always stopped until one night, lying at anchor with the whole crew asleep, he got up on deck unobserved. No one knows what happened, least of all himself, for he woke up in the water swimming for the shore. The cook, as first man up, seeing the empty bunk went on deck and aft to the engine room. Failing to find him, he raised the alarm. The crew dragged round the area for hours with hooks and grapples in an effort to recover his body before marking the spot where they had anchored and making off for the nearest pier to notify the police. It was only then that they learned that their shipmate had swum ashore and reached a crofter's cottage almost exhausted. Luckily he was a strong swimmer, for he swam the best part of a mile, and luckier yet that it was summertime, for he might not have survived the cold even if he had been able to see which direction to go on a dark winter's night. Why he did not swim back to the boat neither he nor anyone else will ever know. I know this man quite well and he does not like to discuss this experience, nor has he ever been back to ring-net fishing again.

The best of these 'mare' stories are told at the ringers' weekly midnight broadcasts which carry on spasmodically until the last of the boats has reached home. Picture the lights of twenty or thirty ring-net boats on a frosty starlight night, when reception is always best, spread over an area of several square miles, leaving the Outer Hebrides for home across the Minch. On Friday nights round about midnight, whether they have herring or not, it is usual for the Minch ring-net fleet to make for home. For the Mallaig boats this is a six- to eight-hour journey which they invariably make together. Since the advent of interboat wireless communication, they can call each other up, using what is referred to as the Trawler Waveband, congregate and set off. As soon as they are under way, the men on watch switch on their wirelesses and the broadcast begins. It invariably starts with an interboat discussion of the night's fishing – who has, and who has not, caught herring, how much and where. It soon develops into a concert of spontaneous variety turns; songs are demanded by all and sundry from some particularly good singer; a variety of the more portable musical instruments ranging from a Jew's harp to a piano accordion are heard from different boats, and Michael, one of the *Spindrift*'s crew, can even produce a set of bagpipes, very much in demand. I have often obliged on both a tin whistle and a mouth-organ. This concert is eagerly listened to by all the fishermen's families for they have a Trawler Waveband on their wireless sets at home. This waveband is a great boon, enabling them to have news of their menfolk at sea. It carries a variety of unofficial messages ranging from 'Father's got ninety cran in Corrodale tonight, Mum,' to 'Don't tease the kitten while I'm away!' I know a Mallaig woman very well whose husband and two sons go to sea together, and from the youngest one every night at eleven o'clock she receives a regular bulletin. He tells her where they are, how much herring they have, if any, and when they expect to be home; it is, of course, impossible for her to reply.

During the war, crews drawn from the fishing fleets did great service in minesweepers; their cool nerve in any situation despite the weather is legendary and even the tremendous losses in the early days of the acoustic mine did little to damp their spirits. They took it all in their stride, for their very existence at sea is one long battle with the elements, and to many of them mines and dive-bombers were just an added hazard.

The Taylor brothers, Buck and Jake, are typical examples. Both are huge, strong, but quiet and unassuming men who fish together in the Fraserburgh ringer *Blairmore*. They remained together during the war, Buck as skipper and Jake as engineer of an old steam drifter minesweeping in the Channel. When their flotilla was attacked by dive-bombers, which sank most of them in the first attack, their drifter was sprayed again and again with machine-gun bullets until, as Buck described it: 'The wheelhoose was hingin' awf.' Despite the pasting they were getting, their old drifter fought back, blazing away for all she was worth and zig-zagging to try and avoid the bombs. Suddenly she got a direct hit aft of the wheelhouse; it struck the raised iron casing over the engine room, but failed to explode. Jake was alone in the engine room firing the boiler when the bomb landed among the coal very nearly in his shovel. He dashed up on deck and into the wheelhouse, where he found his brother still in one piece and doing his best to dodge the bombs that were falling like hail round them. Leaving Buck at the wheel, Jake made for the machine-gun and continued firing at the bombers even after he was badly wounded in the arm, expecting every minute to be blown to kingdom come by the bomb in the engine room, or a near miss with another to stove in their aged planks. When the attack was over and before they circled back to pick up any survivors, they both went down below to see what could be done about the bomb. On closer inspection they found it would fit into the big 'bucket' used for drawing up the ashes to be dumped. Without further ado they manhandled it into the bucket, heaved it up on deck and chucked it over the side. When the remnants of the sweeping patrol returned to their base, and Buck had landed his share of survivors, he was asked the reason for the terrific hole in the casing to which he replied: 'A boom fell doon thru' the casin' an' Jake an' I fir't 't oot ower!' This was not good enough for the base commander, who demanded a written report, and it was only after much persuasion and finally threats that he got it. It must have been a classic worthy of framing, for Buck, who hated fuss of any sort simply wrote down his original remarks. They were both summoned to London to receive decorations but there they met some old shipmates and somehow never arrived at Buckingham Palace.

Then there was old Baldy, a ring-net skipper from the Clyde who has fished in the Minch area as long as anyone can remember. He is well on in his seventies but as strong and active as any of the younger generation. Nothing ever seems to worry him; he is always the same, ready for a joke often at his own expense, and has the happiest disposition I believe I have ever met. He is passion-ately fond of animals and, his own little terrier having died of old age, he acquired in Mallaig a small Cairn-type puppy of dubious parentage. The pup, no bigger than a full-size rat, was brought down to his boat one stormy February morning. Right off he ordered the cook ashore for a pound of the best steak and a pint of fresh milk. This he offered to the puppy – nothing but the best for Baldy's pup; the cook had to cut up the steak into small pieces and then fry it before the dog could be persuaded to eat it. The remainder of the fleet were all away to sea ahead of him, but Baldy would not leave the harbour until his new pet had eaten its fill; the motion of the boat might put it off he said. It was a blustery morning with frequent showers of sleet and on leaving the shelter of the harbour they met some heavy seas. About an hour out of Mallaig the pup began to show signs of distress and wanted to get out of the wheelhouse; when Baldy opened the door, the puppy simply walked aft and fell over the side. Despite the cold and with complete disregard for his own safety old Baldy immediately took the engine out of gear, pulled off his seaboots and dived overboard after it. His crew, below at the time, rushed on deck when they heard the engine eased down so suddenly. They were amazed to find nothing in the wheelhouse but Baldy's boots. Baldy himself was away astern, swimming on his back with his little puppy crouching on his barrel-like chest. On getting up to him, Baldy would not be helped. 'Get the puppy,' he roared, 'get her into a fish-basket!' and it was only when he saw the puppy safely decanted from the basket on to the deck that he would condescend to be helped himself.

Chapter Seven

The following spring, having repaired the damage of the previous season and, we hoped, having profited by our experience, Johnny and I got the *Traveller* once again rigged out for sharkfishing. As we had bought our experience quite dearly, we never again fired at an oncoming shark, but always approached them from the rear. The value of the oil had risen and so correspondingly had the price which we received for the liver, and we went off in high hopes of a record season. We were in operation before our rival of the previous year appeared in the area and for a period had the whole Minch to ourselves. As the season advanced we were to have a positive invasion of far more efficient rivals than any we had yet met.

We were doing very well and often landing cargoes of liver in Mallaig several times a week. As the result of this there appeared in one of the Scottish daily papers a report to the effect that we had landed twenty-three SHARKS in one day, under the heading 'Minch Invaded by Sharks', inserted by an over-zealous local reporter. The impression conveyed to those not in the know was that something of the size of the *Balæna* must be doing very nicely off the West Coast! The immediate result was a real invasion of the Minch area, this time by a horde of Norwegian North Sea whalers, who thought they were on to a good thing. They were – at our expense.

One evening we had come over from Canna to Moonen Bay and finding no sharks there had joined the lobster boat *Winner* at the lighthouse jetty. I had stayed aboard, lying in my bunk reading,

Chapter Seven

but Johnny and the lobstermen went ashore to visit the keepers. I must have dozed off for I was rudely awakened by Jimack, the *Winner*'s skipper, whom I knew very well as we had been to sea together at the ring-net, shouting down the hatch: 'Come awa' noo, Tex, afore the shark jumps in ower!'

This was followed by a tremendous bang on the deck above my head. Sticking my head out of the hatch I saw Johnny rise from all fours, having jumped from the jetty on to the *Traveller*'s foredeck. He shouted to me: 'Start her up, Tex. There's a shark at the stern!'

I heaved myself out on deck and, looking aft, I saw the fish and dived for the engine room. The shark had moved some fifty yards out into the bay by the time we were clear and away. It must have been less than five minutes later that we had a harpoon fast and were being towed out of the bay at the usual rate. The lobstermen had climbed up a little way in order to see the fun and, looking back towards the lighthouse jetty, I could see them obviously enjoying their grandstand view. Johnny and I waved to them as we raced away but as the shark headed for the open sea Neist Point hid them from sight. We allowed the shark to tow us for much longer than we normally did and when we began to tow him we had quite a way to go to get him back to the shelter of the bay. We probably profited by this; for the shark; a very large one, was pretty quiet when brought alongside. We took the liver from the fish straight aboard the boat so that we could tow the carcase out to sea as the ring-net men had asked us to do. That season for greater speed we had hitherto made it a practice, when in deep water, to cut the liver clear of the shark first, when it would float astern of the boat, and to get rid of the shark at once before circling round and brailing the liver aboard. The ring-net men felt that shark carcases might ruin their favourite fishing grounds, for sharks and herring, both being plankton feeders, are frequently to be found together.

With about half the liver on board I was down in the hold putting it into barrels when I heard the unmistakable 'tonk, tonk, tonk' of a Scandinavian single-cylinder diesel, and looked up to see, rounding Neist Point, a lovely Norwegian fishing boat with a huge gun mounted on her stem. She altered course and made straight for us. It must have been quite a surprise for her crew as they saw this wee Scotch boat with a shark alongside almost the length of herself, and its liver coming aboard so easily with only two men. They were even more surprised when we told them we were the only shark-boat in the area, for they had read the newspaper report in Stornoway.

They lay-to until we were finished with the liver, then with the shark still tied to us we hailed them to come alongside. Some of the crew lowered themselves down on to our deck. There was no need for me to air my smattering of Norwegian, learnt from their Linge Company during the war, for they all had fairly good English. They were greatly impressed by what they called our 'cannon' and also our harpoons. Both were much smaller than their own and yet they could see for themselves that the gun was capable of firing our harpoon right through the fish and out the other side, which was all they could ask from any gun. They told us that our method of bringing the liver aboard, though somewhat similar, was much ahead of theirs. They had a huge net 'bucket' and poking the liver into it with long poles entailed quite a performance from such a large boat. She was in fact more than twice as long and at least twice as high out of the water as the *Traveller*. She was called the *Barmøy* and we were to come to know Per Mjetanes, her skipper, and his son Jacob ('Jacko') very well. In fact we had the entire crew to visit us at the weekends when they were in Mallaig. That year and the next we were to encounter scores of Norwegian boats of many types and sizes, but the *Barmøy* I knew best of all, for we fished together several times. I never considered her as a competitor and we helped each other as fishermen should.

These Norwegian boats were between fifty and eighty feet long, all built of wood, and they looked very fine sea-boats. There were Hardanger cutters, straight-stemmed boats with a high sheer and very little freeboard in their waist; there were Möre-type cutters, somewhat similar but which appeared much stronger and were of a more compact construction and with a larger wheel-house. The smallest boats were rather like Colin-Archer-type yachts, they were also cutter-rigged and had a canoe stern and a curved stem, and an external rudder like the *Traveller*. Without exception these boats were powered by single-cylinder semidiesel engines, usually the Swedish Wickman, with a speed of six to eight knots. They were made entirely of fir, but the planking was double; a skin of two and a half to three inches thick on the outside of the ribs and another skin of two to two and a half inches thick on the inside of the ribs. Both inner and outer planking is through-fastened by trenails, wooden pegs driven through and through and wedged inside and outside. This type of construction, although strong, has its drawbacks, for these boats are very prone to dry rot through lack of ventilation.

After we had dumped the carcase we went aboard the *Barmøy* and examined their gun and harpoons. The former was like our own, a muzzle-loader, and the main-charge like mine was ignited by a blank cartridge, but it was twice as big and fired a harpoon which was nothing more nor less than a fluted iron bar about four feet long with the harpoon line made fast to the middle of it. All the Norwegian boats I met carried guns of similar design. The object of the harpoon was to fire it through the fish so that when the strain came on the line the bar turned broadside on as it were, acting as did the barbs on our own harpoon to prevent it pulling out; but, whereas our harpoon did not necessarily have to go right through the fish and out the other side in order to be effective, theirs did.

There were six bunks in the fo'c'sle and a small cabin aft of the wheelhouse, which was vast by local standards. This wheelhouse cabin had accommodation for two men, the skipper and the engin-eer. The galley was aft of this and still part of the wheelhouse and it operated entirely on bottled gas. They had a wireless receiver and transmitter similar to those used by the Scottish herring fleet, but their echo-sounding gear was a more elaborate affair than the type I was used to in ringers. Her bulwarks and superstructure were painted white but the hull was not painted at all, simply dressed with linseed oil. She carried a lifeboat alongside the wheelhouse and this also was painted white. There was a barrel at the top of the mast which served as a crow's nest and the skipper could steer the boat from a second steering wheel on the top of the wheelhouse, where there was a canvas dodger rigged up to afford him shelter. From this height he could keep a shark in view until he was almost up to it and I envied him this, for I was never able to see the shark when I got close up to it.

They had an ingenious arrangement for taking the sudden strain, as they hardly let the shark sound at all. The harpoon line led aboard from the shark through a built-in roller on the point of her nose and passed through a double pulley block about two feet above the deck alongside the mast, and then through a single pulley block halfway up the mast, back down again, and through the other sheave in the double block and from there to the winch just forward of amidships. The double block was attached to a wire rope which disappeared through a small hole in the deck at the foot of the mast. The wire was threaded through a hole in the centre of a block of rubber three feet square suspended just below the deck which was reinforced at that point. This wire was spliced into a three-foot length of permanent-way rail below the rubber. The other block halfway up the mast was attached to a huge steel spring and it was the spring which was actually attached to the mast.

When a shark was harpooned this arrangement enabled them to heave on the winch almost at once, the jerks being taken up on the spring at the top and the lump of rubber at the bottom. They certainly had the sharks to the surface a lot quicker than we did but what they gained on the swings they lost on the roundabout, for their sharks were very much more obstreperous than the majority of ours. It therefore took them much longer to secure the fish in position in order to get at the liver. The time we spent towing our sharks to tire them out was sometimes less than the time they took getting their sharks lashed securely enough to cut them open.

We cruised about the Moonen Bay area for the remainder of the evening but neither we nor the *Barmøy* met any more sharks. We were on our way back into the bay, intending to spend the night alongside the *Winner* at the lighthouse jetty, when the *Barmøy* steamed in and hailed us. She lay-to a boat's length off and Jacob came to the stem-head to tell us that he had heard on his wireless one of the ringers reporting sharks at Eriskay. He knew that we had no wireless set on which we could hear the boats so he had come to pass on the news before setting off across the Minch.

As we already had an almost full cargo, one more shark would fill all our barrels. Under the circumstances it was not worth our while going across so we wished him luck and carried on for the jetty. Next Monday morning, having had corroboration from the ring-net men that there were several large packs of sharks on the other side of the Minch, we set off for Loch Boisdale. The ring-net men had told us that the heaviest concentration of sharks they had met the previous week was from Loch Boisdale in South Uist, southwards.

We met no sharks at Canna, nor in fact until we reached the mouth of Loch Boisdale, where it was questionable which were the more plentiful, sharks or Norwegian shark-boats. We had been wondering for some time, as we steamed towards Loch Boisdale, the reason for the tremendous wheeling canopy of seagulls at the mouth of the loch, for the boats themselves were at that time still hull-down over the horizon. As we drew closer we could hear the WOOMPH of the Norwegian guns and the effect was reminiscent of a sea battle. Up until that time Johnny and I had no idea that there were so many Norwegians in the Minch.

When we came within sight of the island of Uist we counted thirty Norwegian shark-boats along a half-mile stretch of shore around the mouth of Loch Boisdale. They were very busy and competition appeared to be keen among themselves. The sea in the near vicinity was red with blood and the air was alive with countless thousands of seabirds having the gorge of a lifetime on the floating offal. They had obviously cleaned up a fairly considerable pack between them before we arrived and now the entire fleet converged at full speed on every shark that was sighted until we were sure they must collide. Several times we set off in pursuit but the odds were enormous and we had neither the size nor the power to compete. Not that we retired empty-handed, for we got one shark, but even that was only ours because it rose inshore of us and the Norwegians never saw it. I could not see the *Barmøy* among the fleet, so after we had finished taking the liver from our shark we cleared off south where we hoped there might still be some sharks. We were lucky in this, for we met only four Norwegians farther to the south'ard. Off Eriskay we met them fishing and as there were sometimes more sharks showing on the surface than there were boats we held our own.

O'Connor protested vigorously about the Norwegians and later that season I met not only him but also Harry Thompson, the latter now fishing on his own. Although both of them, unlike us, rendered down their liver at sea, I did not think this any financial advantage to a small sharkfishing venture and considered it a hindrance when they had to compete with the Norwegians. I remembered meeting O'Connor in Scalpay, Harris, and recalled thinking then that his floating 'factory', a thirty-foot steel lifeboat, which he had to tow, tended to slow him down and render him dependent on a shore base. Weighing it all up, and bearing in mind that his boat had the same engine as the *Traveller* but was slower, I felt that he was in no better case than we were as far as competition with the Norwegians was concerned. Furthermore, O'Connor's overheads must have amounted to considerably more than our own, for he had to tow his sharks in, beach them, employ men to take out the liver, and then ferry it out to the 'factory' in a dinghy. He also had a crew of four in his catcher as opposed to the two of us.

Harry Thompson's factory was a forty-foot fishing boat, and

his catcher a first-class launch about the length of the *Traveller*. She was a little faster than either of us and both Harry's boats were capable of moving about. In fact, the quarters for the crews of both boats were in the factory boat, where all four men slept.

On one occasion when we went into Scalpay for the night and found O'Connor still there, we went to see how he was getting on. He told us that the *Scottish Daily Express* was sending up a man by plane to take photographs of the Norwegian sharkfishing fleet. He also told me that he had been in touch with the Fishery Division at St Andrew's House and had asked them to send up a cruiser to protect his interests. There is no doubt that the Norwegians were fishing within the three-mile limit and he hoped that the photographer would obtain proof of this. He wanted us to stay in harbour and add weight to his arguments and added that we would have our pictures in the papers. I replied that we had had enough publicity and it had gained us nothing.

Next morning we went out again and managed to hold our own amongst the Norwegians but as the season was drawing to a close we fished farther northwards.

There is no doubt that O'Connor was justified in drawing attention to what was in fact an act of poaching, but the position was a peculiar one. Legally the Norwegian fishermen were in the wrong, although one could hardly blame them. They had started to come down from Norway to fish in the Minch because Norwegian boats visiting their consulate in Stornoway were bound to meet the local drift-net herring fleet, who begged them to shoot a few of the basking sharks which played such havoc with their nets. All the larger Norwegian boats carry guns for whales. Nor were the herring fishermen the only ones who suffered, for I know that sharks also did considerable damage to the salmon bag-nets at the little salmon station on Soay, and when the sharks were particularly plentiful the salmon fishers were forced to take their nets ashore. There is no reason to believe that this did not apply equally to other salmon stations in the area. Quite apart from the initial damage, even after the net was mended the parts which had come in contact with the shark continued to rot away. The fishermen blame some corrosive element in the black slime with which the shark is covered. Incidentally, as I know from unpleasant experience on several occasions, this slime entering through an almost microscopic wound can cause rapid and serious blood-poisoning and we always had a tin of antiphlogistine in the medicine chest for immediate application.

As far as I know these Norwegians were the first sharkfishing boats the Stornoway herring fleet had ever met. At the time of O'Connor's protests the only Scottish shark-boats were himself, Harry Thompson's and the *Traveller*. It was about this time that the International Conference at The Hague resulted in the loss to us of certain fishing grounds off the coast of Norway, and also that King Haakon was on a State Visit to London. It is therefore not surprising that the authorities seemed reluctant to act in response to O'Connor's pleas to have the Norwegians chased back to Norway. It may be, too, that the interests of the herring fleet were considered of more importance than those of a small sharkfishing boat. In north-west Scotland the herring industry is a very important one, employing a great number of men and women, and basking sharks have been one of the fishermen's greatest headaches from time immemorial.

We ended that season fishing off Lewis, going into Stornoway every night where we unloaded our barrels of liver. The Outer Hebrides steamer carried them to Mallaig and brought back empties for us. We, who had hitherto had to make for Mallaig every time our liver barrels were full, found fishing out of Stornoway to be money for old rope. Elsewhere we had so often been forced to leave a pack of sharks because the liver barrels were full.

One of the things that sticks in my mind about Stornoway is the new Seamen's Mission, which at that time was apparently not officially open. Nevertheless, this was the only place in the Hebrides where we could enjoy the luxury of a bath at any time we wanted. We were not the only ones to seize the opportunity when we found it existed, for I often met Jacob Mjetanes and the crew of the *Barmøy* there, and some of the other Norwegians whom I did not know so well.

During the three weeks we fished there we never had to look very far for sharks; in fact, we usually left the harbour between seven and eight in the morning, when the local herring fleet on their way in with their catch were only too pleased to tell us where the sharks were. On our way out one morning when we were abreast of the lighthouse at the entrance to the harbour both Johnny and I were startled by a shark leaping clean out of the water some 200 yards ahead of us. From this distance it appeared that the shark must have been some eight feet from the surface at the height of his leap. Within the minute he was airborne again and in fact he repeated this performance four times before disappearing beneath the surface. It was hardly a graceful manœuvre, producing sheets of spray and a resounding crack as he hit the water with his whole length. It is a pity that the scientists who stated so categorically that basking sharks are incapable of leaping clear of the water were not with us then. They could have seen for themselves that the fishermen on whose combined testimony they were forced to withdraw this erroneous statement were not exaggerating. As far as I know the only one of them who ever actually went sharkfishing was Dr Harrison Mathews, who spent several days with me. On one occasion he and I had caught a shark from the *Gannet*, Maxwell's small catcher, and he was as good a crew as I ever had, but unfortunately the sharks did not put on a performance like this for him. I had often seen sharks do this but I was never nearer to a shark in the air than I was by the time this one made his fourth leap.

We hung about waiting for him to surface again and within about a quarter of an hour there were four or five sharks showing. We made for the nearest one and, finding it to be a good hefty fish, harpooned it. We allowed it to tow us right out to sea, clear of the incoming boats, before starting to work it. This shark put up a magnificent fight and we had to tow him for the best part of an hour before we were able to get him to come to the surface. When at last we managed to winch him up to the side of the boat his efforts to break loose were dangerously spectacular. At this stage of the proceedings the shark is invariably boring down for all he is worth and frantic tail-lashing is what we expect. Instead of this, this fellow came clean out of the water, head-first, as if he was chased by all the devils of the deep. The sudden strain caused by this unexpected manœuvre almost pulled the winch out of the boat, for the shark had caught me unawares and I was forced to pay out rope and let him sound again. He was brought to the surface again, only to repeat his earlier performance. This time he leapt several times and during one of his leaps I saw the harpoon lying across his belly. It had passed right through the fish. I had visions of him landing on deck and smashing the boat into smith-ereens, so I threw the turns off the winch barrel and allowed him to sound again. Both Johnny and I were certain that this must be the shark whose leaps had attracted our attention in the first place. We all but lost him when I took the rope off the winch for it ran out at a terrific rate, running through our hands at such a speed that it burnt them before we were able to check it.

When we had it fast we saw that less than half the harpoon rope remained on board. We let him tow us around for about a quarter of an hour but he towed us neither fast nor far in any direction and as he showed no signs of tiring we set the engine off full speed astern to give him more weight to tow. This soon slowed him up and in a short while stopped our forward way altogether. Soon we were moving stern-first, towing the shark with us. The harpoon rope was easily transferred to the winch, for I set the boat away full speed ahead, thereby giving Johnny all the slack he wanted, and we started heaving him up. This time the shark offered very little resistance. Heaving him up was as easy as heaving in our anchor, and as quickly as I can write it Johnny had a wire lasso round his tail.

Transferring the wire to the winch, we heaved the tail right out of the water up flush with our stem, and setting the boat away brought his head alongside aft. There was no difficulty getting the grinda-hook into his jaw and lashing him tight to the boat. The shark was so quiet that I could have sworn he was dead and we set to at once to cut him open. We had filled three barrels with his liver when the fish suddenly seemed to come to life, rolling right over and presenting his back to us. Thinking that the fish must be dead and that this turning was merely a nervous reflex we tried to turn him belly-up again with a boat-hook, for we figured there were at least another three barrels of liver in him. Instead of turning back and remaining belly-up, he kept turning over and over, and entangled the lasso wire in his tail so that each successive turn brought him higher up the boat's side. The *Traveller* rapidly took on a frightening list and with the deck approaching the almost vertical it was impossible to stay aboard without hanging on to something. My one thought then was to get rid of him quickly before he had us over. Jumping for the stem, I snatched up the cleaver which was kept beneath the gun-mounting for such an emergency. With one blow I cut the wire on the rail and as the shark's tail flopped back into the water the boat righted herself. I did not get time to straighten up before the shark began lashing out again. He caught me a terrific wallop on the shoulder, knocked the cleaver out of my hand and sent me spinning up against the wheelhouse. Johnny, farther aft than I, and out of range of the tail, started to say something which was cut short when he in turn was hit, but by the stomach, which burst like a rotten tomato, covering him from head to foot with red plankton. The cuts we had made had released the entrails and odd sections of the internal works came flying through the air after the tail. Johnny had been caught, fair and square, for he had learned to dodge the latter as it came crashing down on the rail, and had become so adept at this while putting on the lasso wire that he merely side-stepped or leaned back a little, like a skilful matador. He had been so busy exercising his skill tail-dodging that he was totally unprepared for this secondary attack. Neither of us was hurt, but before we gathered ourselves together the shark pulled the grinda-hook out of his jaw

and we saw him swimming away on the surface at what we estimated to be eight or ten knots, apparently oblivious that all his
innards were trailing after him. Perhaps I should have felt sorry for
him, but basking sharks are so primitive that they seem not to
belong to the world of creatures which feel pain. As I watched
him go I could not help laughing at Johnny's classical language –
it would have made a bargee envious. He for one certainly was not
sorry for the shark.

Before we could attempt to harpoon another shark we had to
clean up the boat, for the stomach, when it burst across Johnny's
chest, had covered not only him but most of the deck as well with
slimy, half-digested plankton. A slippery deck is not desirable in
any boat but it can be more than dangerous when sharkfishing. We
sloshed copious quantities of water about and brushed it over the
side but this did not improve things much. Rather to the reverse,
I am convinced it made it worse, so we gave it up, coiled down our
harpoon rope and set off in search of another shark.

The remainder of the pack having disappeared, we carried on
north and on rounding Tiumpan Head found ourselves among the
largest school of killer whales (orca gladiator) I had ever seen in my
life. There must have been about twenty of them and they began at
once to circle round the boat in a leisurely way, keeping a respectable distance, but nevertheless there was no doubt that we were
under observation. Killers are the terror of the sea, and although we
sometimes saw other small whales of comparable size, we could
always recognize them as they came up to blow by the distinctive
white blaze on each side of the head, just behind the eye. They are
the largest of the dolphin family but unlike the rest of the species,
which are normally harmless creatures, killers are, without a doubt,
the most ferocious beasts known on land or sea.

Black above and white below, they are beautifully streamlined
and are reputed to be capable of a speed of more than twenty-five
knots. The cow and immature bull killer have a small and slightly
backward-curving dorsal fin, seldom more than 2 feet high. An
old bull has a colossal dorsal fin, as straight as a sword, and because

of this characteristic old-time whalemen referred to them as 'swordfish'. Although their natural habitat is the Arctic and the Antarctic they are also to be found in temperate waters. In the British Isles they are more often encountered off the West Coast of Scotland, in Hebridean waters, than anywhere else. In every school I ever saw there was always one old bull whose sword-like dorsal fin rose much higher out of the water than the rest. The bull we saw that day had the largest dorsal fin I ever saw and I would put it between six and eight feet high. I have never actually seen a killer whale killing anything but I have often seen basking sharks with terrible wounds which I imagine could be inflicted by no other creature in this area. I can remember one shark we unsuccessfully stalked on several days off Uishnish Light in South Uist. Half of his dorsal fin was missing and the tattered shreds of skin and raw flesh showed that the wound was recent.

Killers hunt in packs like wolves and with their highly developed brain and cunningly planned joint attack they are fearsome brutes which will attack man if given half a chance. Ponting, the photographer on Captain Scott's Antarctic Expedition, was fortunate to escape with his life when a school of killer whales began to break up the two-and-a-half-foot-thick ice-floe on the edge of which he was standing. No marine fish or animal is safe from them, not even the largest of whales. Although a bull killer hardly ever exceeds thirty feet in length and a cow less than half that, they kill even the blue whales, which may weigh 100 tons and measure as many feet in length. When a school of killers meet a whale they all move into the attack, like a squadron of fighters harassing a huge bomber. Darting in and out, they rip bits out of it, and if in desperation the whale turns and opens its mouth, one of them rushes in and rips out its tongue and the whale quickly bleeds to death. Killers, and in fact all whales, have their tail flukes set horizontally, as opposed to fish where the tail is set in a vertical plane; this enables them to go astern when they get their teeth into anything and is obviously a great help to them when tearing a huge whale apart. They are reputed to use an ingenious method to get at a seal which imagines itself safe on an ice-floe. They work in unison to make the floe rock or tip it over, and if the floe is too big they even mount it and scare the seal to the other end where there is always another killer waiting to grab it.

We followed the school all morning, trying to get within range to harpoon one, but they were too clever for us. Every time we expected them to rise and blow just ahead of us they cheated us by rising just at our stern. There they remained on the surface with their heads just out of the water, reminiscent of seals, until we turned the boat, when down and away they would go again. It may be worth recording that I never ever saw a shark on the surface any time when there were killers about. I learned that year that all the Norwegian shark boats carried big rifles for no other purpose than destroying these brutes whenever they met them. They told me this was easily done for all they had to do was draw blood to incite the latent cannibalism in the school. The action snowballs, for the more the killers fight over the wounded one the more become wounded and one shot may mean several fewer killers by the end of the mêlée. However, when I applied to the police for a permit to carry a .303 rifle for their destruction, so little is their presence realized that my application was refused. It is therefore interesting to note that it is now suggested (1959) that the gradual increase of killer whales is largely responsible for a corresponding decrease in the seal numbers in the Minch area. I am sure that the police authorities did not then believe that we were likely to meet anything sufficiently dangerous to warrant the use of a big rifle.

The killers eventually cleared off out into the open Minch and we carried on north but encountered no more sharks until the evening, when, on our way south again, we fell in with a dozen or so not far from where we had met the killers that morning. It was obvious that the sharks were swimming high in the water for from some distance off we could clearly see the nose, dorsal fin, and tail all on the surface at one time. We steamed full speed in among them and selected the biggest fish, a huge, thickset male of approximately thirty feet. He remained on the surface until we were right alongside, giving Johnny a perfect opportunity to place his harpoon exactly where he wanted it. The shark was strong and towed us for some considerable distance out to sea before we were able to reverse the process and begin to tow him. Even with the engine going full speed ahead we were towed seawards stern-first, although not very fast, for about half an hour; then, as the shark showed no sign of tiring, we decided to brew some tea. Leaving Johnny in the wheelhouse to keep an eye on things, I made for the fo'c'sle where I quickly had the kettle boiling. I did not get as far as making the tea, for my preparations were rudely interrupted by Johnny's stentorian bellows and the sudden easing of the engine to dead slow. Dropping everything I bolted on deck to be greeted by Johnny shouting: 'Get your camera, Tex. The shark is jumping out of the water like the Loch Ness Monster!'

I saw at once what was happening. Instead of struggling to get away, the shark was now coming with us, swimming on the surface parallel to the boat. Every now and then his tail would rear out of the water, followed by almost half the body, and for a second he appeared to be standing on his head, only to bend like a bow as the tail slapped back into the water. This was too good to miss, so, shouting to Johnny to keep the boat going in case the fish got ahead of us and put the harpoon rope in the propeller, I jumped back down into the fo'c'sle to fetch my camera. Johnny had by this time set the boat away full speed, and as I expected the shark to resurface astern of us I ran aft to the wheelhouse to be as near the fish as possible while taking the photograph. I did not get there; for the deck being still slippery with the stomach contents of the first shark, I skidded, my feet hit the rail and I plunged head-first right over the stern, camera and all. I made a grab at the harpoon rope but missed it and when I came to the surface the boat was some thirty yards away. My first thought on hitting the water was of the killer whales, and I hoped that they were not within sight of us. The harpoon rope was quite near to me so I struck out for it for all I was worth, shouting to Johnny to ease down but not to stop altogether, as I did not want to be too close to the shark, should it continue breaching as it had been doing. I was soon up to the rope and got a firm grip of it with both hands and began hauling myself towards the boat. When Johnny saw me hanging on to the rope he set the engine off full speed again, for although I did not see it, the fish was coming up fast behind me. The speed with which the boat took up the slack almost swept me away and I was forced to allow the rope to slip through my hands when the strain on my arms became too much for me; by the time Johnny was able to ease down the engine I was much nearer the shark. Again I set off hand over hand pulling myself towards the boat, but it could not have been many seconds before I was yanked clean out of the water as the shark broke surface again; still I hung on, only to be slapped down on the water like a wet rag. My feet were touching the shark's back before I managed to gather myself together and I felt myself being swept through the water at a terrific rate. When at last I was able to take stock of things I could see that Johnny had given the *Traveller* all she had got to straighten out the rope but now she appeared to be stopped. This time I made good progress and was soon able to keep my head above water, for the strain on the rope kept it well above the surface. It was at this juncture that I saw Johnny leave the wheelhouse, run to the gunmounting, pick up the cleaver and hurry aft. I prayed hard that he, too, would not slip on the deck and follow me into the water. By the time he was back at the aft towing post I was near enough to yell to him not to cut the rope for I was determined to have this fish after the bother it was causing me. I was soon up to the *Traveller*'s stern, where Johnny had hung a motor tire for me to get a grip of, but before he was able to help me aboard he was obliged to set the boat away ahead again, for the fish broke surface too close to our stern. Johnny soon yanked me aboard and I stripped off right down to my birthday suit, for the sun was still up and it was quite warm.

'What about that cup of tea, Tex? You'll need it now!' was the only remark he made as he jumped back to the wheelhouse the moment he had me aboard.

The shark gradually stopped its antics until at last, giving up the ghost, it allowed us to tow it where we wished. It was easy enough to handle, for there was very little life in it when we winched it up alongside. Nevertheless, it yielded nine barrels of liver. Later that evening we managed to harpoon another small shark which yielded only four barrels. We saw no more of the killer whales on our way south to Stornoway, where we landed our sixteen barrels that night.

Before that season ended it had become increasingly obvious that if we were to hold our own amongst so many Norwegians we must either get a larger boat or give the *Traveller* more power. Johnny and I discussed this question at length, many times. A larger boat would require more men, an idea which appealed to neither of us and one which might not add to our efficiency. Whereas, if the *Traveller* could steam as fast as the Norwegian boats when racing for a shark, we would certainly catch our share. We had repeatedly found that we two could handle a shark as well as any Norwegians, once we had actually harpooned it. The session that we had had at the mouth of Boisdale Loch had shown us that it was speed we required above all.

I took my query to old 'Harry' Manson, Jim's father and the patriarch skipper of the Mallaig ring-net fleet. His advice was: 'Stick to the wee boat, Tex. You're doing OK as you are. If the Norwegian boats can beat you, get a bigger engine. I'm sure your boat can carry it.'

He reasoned, as Johnny and I had, that bigger boats mean more men, and more men need more money, and that we might find ourselves working twice as hard for half as much. Furthermore, what were we to do with a larger boat for the rest of the year? The *Traveller* could go to the lobsters with any size of engine.

As soon as the season was over I put the *Traveller* on to the slip at Mallaig for an extensive overhaul. She was fitted with a new stem and keel and several new planks to replace those on her bottom which had been badly scored by harpoons. After the carpenters had finished with her and she had been scraped and repainted, she looked like a new boat.

The old paraffin engine was taken out and in its place went a forty-four hp diesel. The old engine had served us very well, and had shifted the *Traveller* at a reasonable speed, even although several of the original twenty-six horses had long since died of old age. Both Johnny and I were itching to see her afloat again, for we felt sure that, if everything bore equal strain, she would fly with this new engine.

All this work took most of the winter and therefore Johnny and I were again unable to use the *Traveller* to go to the lobsters. Nevertheless we did go lobster-fishing, when an unexpected opportunity presented itself.

It could not have been long after the *Traveller* went on to the slip that Jim Sutherland, 'Jimack' of the *Winner*, came up to Glasnacardoch one Sunday evening. He needed someone to take his boat while he and his nephew went 'home' for a wedding, and I was the only skipper he knew who was not at sea. He also inquired whether Johnny would take the place of his nephew, who was the third member of the crew. I readily agreed for a multitude of reasons, chief among them that I was very fond of old Jimack.

A small, lively man, then in his late sixties, he was full of fun and possessed of a puckish sense of humour. He had not long retired from the sea when he surprised everyone by buying a share in the *Winner*. He had been her skipper for many years when she was ring-net fishing and maybe it was sentiment that prompted him to go back to her, for he knew little about lobster fishing and cared less, and was the first to admit it. All that Jimack wanted was to be among the boats. His partner, big Willie 'Uskavagh', who came from the place of that name in Benbecula, was the exact opposite. A large, solemn man, never given to optimism or over-enthusiasm, but who knew lobster fishing from A to Z.

As we had no intimate knowledge of the technique of lobster fishing, this was a golden opportunity for both of us to study the expert at work.

Chapter Seven

We left Mallaig early Monday morning and steamed north, through the sound of Sleat, up the back of Skye and through the sound between Raasay and Rona, and right up to Ru Hunish, the northernmost tip of Skye. The *Winner*, as is the local custom, carried three men, one the skipper, one to work the winch and the other to take the creels aboard. The Mallaig boats usually work about 200 creels. These are shaped like Nissen huts, thirty inches long, eighteen inches wide, and fifteen inches high. The bottom is made of wooden slats nailed across two thirty-inch runners and the framework of the 'hut' consists of three hazel hoops or bows, set into these runners, with three straight hazel sticks to join them together at the top and shoulders of the bows. This framework is covered with a net made of heavy twine and there is an eye ring at either side of the creel to allow the lobsters to go in, but set into a sleeve of net in such a way that it is difficult for them to get out again.

They are left on the fishing grounds over the weekend and rebaited or shifted on Monday to start the week. On reaching Ru Hunish we steamed close inshore and prepared to pick up the first of our ends, inflatable buoys from which a line leads down to the first of the fleet of twenty creels. We took up our stations, myself remaining in the wheelhouse, Willie going to the winch and Johnny, armed with a boat-hook, picked up the buoy and hauled the line aboard. The line was passed through a roller in the boat's side and on to the winch barrel and Willie began heaving. The creels, arranged along this main line at ten-fathom intervals, are attached to it by side ropes about a fathom long. When the first creel reached the boat's side it was Johnny's job to grab it and haul it aboard, take out the lobsters, if any, throw away the old bait and replace it with fresh. The bait is generally a whole salted mackerel, slipped in between two strings which run from the top of the middle bow to the flat stone which is tied on top of the slats in the creel as a sinker. This done, the creel is placed as far forrard on the foredeck as is possible and by the time this has been done the next creel is coming to the rail, and so on, until the whole fleet has been rebaited. The lobsters are put into a box on deck and when the fleet has been hauled the tendons on each claw are cut to prevent them killing each other. This is a very simple operation: the lobster, held by the back, is placed against a piece of hardwood screwed on to the wheelhouse for the purpose, which it catches in its claws, thereby exposing the joint in the shell and the tendon can be nicked with a sharp knife. As the weather was calm we were able to take all ten fleets aboard at once. As the *Winner* is only forty feet long, you can well imagine what she looked like; shut in my wheelhouse I could see nothing, but Johnny perched on top of the mountain of creels kept me right.

I had heard that the Shiant Islands were a good place for lobsters and, as I knew them, Willie decided we should try them. Situated some five miles east of Harris are the three small islands Garbh, Eilean Mhuire and Eilean an Tigh, whose combined area is about five hundred acres and their highest point over five hundred feet. The tremendous columnar architecture of the tertiary basalt on the north face of Garbh is said to be the most impressive example in Scotland, but the Shiants are difficult to land on and seldom visited except by an occasional lobster fisherman. They are uninhabited except for a few weeks in summer when some shepherds come over from Harris to attend to the sheep. They live in a small stone cottage on Eilean an Tigh. The islands are infested with brown rats which do pretty well for themselves in the spring when they must severely depredate the nesting colonies of the breeding sea birds, feeding first on eggs and then on the young as they hatch, but I think their staple food must be shellfish. I do not think that rats are much of a menace to the larger gulls, for some years ago I had a young Greater Blackback with a broken wing; kept aboard a fishing boat which was over-run with rats it was not long before the young gull cleared them all out of her. I have watched that gull catch and kill a rat and instantaneously swallow it. Even a limpet can be a match for a careless rat, for I once saw a rat drowned by one. It had been trying to get at the limpet with its tongue but the limpet had clamped down on it and held it there until the tide came in and drowned it.

As soon as we arrived we shot our creels. It was my job to steer the boat slowly in and out among the reefs and all along the shore, sowing creels as we went. As we steamed along, Johnny stood on deck to watch that the lobster line ran freely and that each successive creel to be pitched over the side was selected from the mountain at the right moment. Willie had to be watching in the stem, directing me with shouts of 'shady in' or out, port or starboard as the case might be, for as it was low water we were laying the creels as close inshore as we dared. It would never do to get into trouble out here, for if we were to run the boat on to a rock there would be very little chance of getting help for days, maybe weeks, since no one knew where we were, and by that time the boat would be in bits.

In the evening we hauled them again and the lobsters we had caught were packed in boxes and the lids nailed down. These boxes, which have a great number of inch-and-a-half holes bored in them, are arranged like a fleet of creels except that to the ends of the line are fastened anchors instead of buoys, for of course the boxes float. Before we went to our anchor for the night we shot the boxes some little distance away; the holes allow the free passage of water through them and also ensure that nothing but the lid is above the surface, for if the lobsters were to remain too long out of water they would die. This latter is the lobster fisherman's greatest bogey because of the colossal percentage of lobsters that die before they reach the market, especially in hot summer weather. It is illegal for a fisherman to sell a dead lobster because of the danger of fish poisoning.

We continued to fish round the Shiants for the rest of the week, hauling the creels twice a day. We caught a tremendous number of lobsters, no doubt because the Skye fishermen seldom attempt to fish here as there is very little shelter from most winds and, if a gale did blow up, they would be forced to clear out leaving all their gear, which in all probability would be smashed up by the swell.

As we were a good number of hours from Mallaig we stopped twice on our way home and put the boxes of lobsters over the side to revive them and, although there were a number of casualties, we still managed to send a thousand pounds live weight of lobsters to Billingsgate, and for this we received a shilling a pound. Maybe you wonder, like I do, why they are so expensive by the time they reach the fishmonger's slab.

Chapter Eight

The first fall of snow saw me back again at Meoble, helping John the stalker with the hind-shooting. When I arrived I found a far heavier fall than that which I had left at Mallaig, and there were some sizeable drifts on the Meoble road. All this snow brought to mind the deer calves that we used to find stranded in snowdrifts quite close to the road, and how during the war Duncan and I carried them home on our backs and hid them in his barn among bales of hay until they grew strong enough to be turned loose again when the snow had gone. Sometimes when the snow was long in going they became quite tame and refused to go away when we turned them loose. His wife used to give us beano when this happened, for, she complained, it was bad enough trying to keep wild deer out of the garden without us bringing them home and taming them. There was one hind called 'Tex's hind' which was known by everyone on the estate. She used to come right into the byre with Duncan on winter mornings to get her hay ration along with his cattle. He told me that she had had a calf with her the previous year but that she had not put in an appearance that winter so far. I was sorry to learn later that she never returned. Probably she trusted too many men and fell somewhere to a poacher's rifle.

We had some very fine days on the hill together, but I must thank Bessie, one of John's beautifully trained dogs, for the best hind of the season.

One morning we awoke to find the snow mostly all gone, for it had been raining in the night. It is very difficult to see hinds when the ground is *breac* (Gaelic for speckled), as John called it. The hinds would be feeding on the patches with no snow and then they seem darker than they really are. Somehow our eyes are never as good under these conditions, for we are probably dazzled by the snow and cannot pick out the detail on the darker patches. Nevertheless, off I went as early as I could, down the hill and over the bridge, to John's house to see what he thought of the prospects.

The river had grown in the night and was now a raging torrent of brown, peaty water. Great rafts of white froth swirled round and round in the eddies at the edge of the great pool below the bridge. I stood for a moment or two, leaning on the handrail, fascinated by the power of the water as it rushed past me. Many a quiet summer's evening had I spent fishing when the river was low, trying to outwit the wary brown trout lying in the broken water at the head of this same pool.

I was in luck; John was for going to the hill. He planned to take a rowing boat and go up the lochside a bit until we saw some hinds on the side of Druim a Chuirn,[1] then go ashore where we thought we could get 'in on them'. There is a fair bit of birch scrub on the side of the hill and we expected to see some hinds there. Before leaving his house John called his little sheep–dog, Bessie, saying he was taking her with us. This did not please me at all.

'Surely the last thing on earth to take stalking with you is a sheep–dog, John?' I said.

'Ach, she'll be quiet enough, Tex; she might even be useful,' he replied.

I had more sense than to argue with him, John would never argue anyway, but I could not understand how a collie dog was going to be useful when we were crawling in on a stalk, and I had little hope of getting a shot that day. On the way up the loch John seemed to be more interested in sheep than deer, which made me wonder if we would end by rounding up some of them to shift them to more sheltered ground, for I could think of no other

1 Gaelic: 'Ridge of Cairns'.

reason for having the dog aboard with us. As I rowed up the loch, John sat in the stern, his dog at his feet, searching the hill with his telescope. Now and again he would remark about a bunch of sheep he could see, but never a word about hinds. At last he closed his glass with a snap, shot it into the leather case he always carried slung across his back, and said: 'We'll go ashore here', pointing ahead to a burn that was plunging down the side of the hill, swollen to twice its usual volume with the melting snow. There was too much water coming down to take the boat in to the mouth of the burn, so we landed a little way from it and hauled the boat well up out of the water.

There was very little wind down at the lochside, but we could see the clouds moving slowly northwards – there would probably be more wind when we got up a bit. This burn had gouged a deep gully for itself during the countless years that it had been flowing down to the loch. It afforded us grand cover on our way up the hill, its steep sides hiding us completely from any beast on the face of the hill unless from directly above us. We scrambled up over loose rocks, leaping from rock to rock in the bed of the burn when the sides were too steep for us. When we had climbed about two thirds of the way up we cautiously emerged from our gully and had a good spy with our telescopes away upwind towards the head of the loch.

One gets a magnificent view from here on a clear day such as this was, with the loch away below us. Right across on the other side we could follow the track which leads down to the sea at Tarbet Bay, Loch Nevis. We had climbed above the birch scrub, so we were not surprised to see no hinds on the side of this bleak and windswept hill.

Eventually we moved off again, this time along the side of the hill, very carefully now with John leading, his dog following so closely behind him that I felt sure that one of these times he would clout it under the chin with his heel; perhaps it was wishful thinking, for the dog judged things better than I expected, nor had it so far made any noise, as I had feared it might. We had gone about a mile when we came upon a mass of huge square rocks, left I suppose by a glacier. We were very wary now, for any one of these rocks could have screened a bunch of hinds; John would go forward and cautiously peep round the side of a particular rock and signal me to follow and off we would go again to another rock. One of the times he peeped over the top of the rock he had crawled to, he instantaneously dropped back, signalling me with his hand to get down. When I crawled up to him, he whispered that there was a fine-looking yeld hind about 300 yards away on the other side of a gully similar to that up which we had originally come. 'I am sure she has not seen us,' he said. He had another look at her and whispered, 'She's feeding. Come on.'

We crawled forward another twenty-five yards or so to another, smaller rock; the dog was the only thing that worried me, for this time for some unknown reason it allowed me to precede it and I could no longer keep my eye on it. We crawled forward fairly fast, for we thought that the hind could have seen us had she lifted her head from feeding, but all went well and we gained our new cover. The dog must have been as close to me as she could possibly get, for she reached the rock at the same moment as I did and lay down tight against John. This cheered me up, for she seemed to know the game well. John slowly pulled the rifle out of the leather case and loaded it, taking care that there was no tell-tale click as the cartridges were inserted. He handed the rifle to me, saying: 'Away you go, Tex; your eyes are younger than mine. We will wait here until we hear your shot.'

I took a quick look at the hind and saw that I would have to crawl forward from rock to rock until I got within range. I could see her quietly feeding on the other side of a burn just as John had said; then it happened. Out of the burn and into full view of me came a sheep. She immediately saw us and indicated her annoy-ance by making that whistling noise they make when startled. I felt John's huge hand on my shoulder pressing me down and back out of her sight. He whispered something in Gaelic to his dog, who at once began to crawl away back the way we had come. It was amazing to watch the way she crawled, her belly tight to the ground; she seemed to be hauling herself forward by her forelegs. More amazing still was the way she made use of the cover; one would think she had mapped her route out in her head before-hand. She was quickly gone from our sight and I asked John what she was up to.

'We'll watch in a moment or two when she has had time to work her way back again below us,' he replied with a quiet smile. I was itching to have another look over the top of our rock, but I was afraid to spoil whatever stunt John and Bessie were up to. It seemed ages before John indicated that we were to have a look, only this time we were not to look over the top but round the sides and as low as possible. What I saw seemed incredible; the sheep was standing staring at Bessie who had placed herself stra-tegically between it and the hind. She was lying in front of a boulder where the sheep could see her but the hind could not. The sheep appeared to be hypnotized, for it made no move until Bessie began to crawl slowly towards it; she had not crawled five yards when the sheep turned and ran towards us and away past us, paying not the slightest attention to the human intruders. Bessie crawled back a little way and disappeared from our view. The hind, being startled by the sudden exit of the sheep, stopped feeding and gazed all round, but was mostly concerned in looking away from us, no doubt wondering what the sheep had seen beyond her. Satisfying herself that there was nothing to be seen or scented upwind – she could not see us and she obviously had not been able to see Bessie – she resumed feeding, probably thinking, as I do, that sheep are the most foolish things that ever came out of the Ark. In a few moments Bessie was back, repeating her earlier per-formance of crawling the last twenty-five yards and back up to John with never a sound out of her during the whole of this time. John just laid his hand on her and she lay as though dead, seeming not to expect any recognition or reward.

'What on earth did you say to her?' I asked in perplexity.

'Och, I don't need to tell her, she knows that we are here for hinds and not sheep,' he replied. I vowed there and then that the next time we went stalking together I would suggest he take her with us.

I did not sit there long but crawled forward on my stalk as originally intended, all the while keeping my eyes on the hind, only moving when she was feeding and determined to shoot at once should she see me. At last I got to a small boulder about seventy-five yards from the hind; I do not remember how long I took over this but I do remember that I was very wet, the snow had worked down my neck and accumulated round my belt, and my fingers were stiff with cold from sliding the rifle through the snow. From this vantage point I quietly poked my rifle over the top, first of all making sure that the barrel was not plugged up with snow. It was a fine position for a shot; I could kneel and use the boulder as a rest for my left hand. I shot her clean, right through the neck – a beautiful shot, as John later said.

As soon as John heard the shot, he appeared from behind his rock and quickly bled the hind and gralloched it. It was in excellent condition, judging by the mass of fat round the kidneys. We then began to drag it down the hill to the lochside; when we were halfway down John struck off diagonally towards the boat, and I was left on my own to get it down as near the boat as possible. One must be careful when dragging a carcase for, when the going is steep, it is apt to roll over and come charging down behind you, knocking your feet from under you with disastrous results. In very steep places it is best not to go straight down, but rather on a slant, placing yourself to one side of the carcase, according to which way you want to go; then, taking a firm grip of the forelegs, allow it to roll down in a semicircle, coming to rest below you and a little to one side. Sometimes it is not so easy; for you may find that you have to go uphill for a start, which requires no particular skill, just brute strength. It is best to drag a hind by its forefeet and the lay of the coat will help it to slip over the ground. Some stalkers use a rope, but I never did. With this the two front feet are tied together and stretched out forward; the rope is then passed through a cut

which is made in the lower jaw, just behind the front teeth, which
keeps the head from flopping all over the place and getting caught
up in stones or similar obstructions. The thing we tried to avoid
most of all was letting it go altogether in a steep place so that it
careered downhill, to fall over something and break its back. It is
very difficult to skin a beast with a broken back, and its carcase,
when hanging in the larder, has an ugly shape which makes it difficult to cut up. This was an easy drag, for it was not so steep when
I got down a bit; just a gentle slope to the side of the loch. I did
not have long to wait for John to arrive with our rowing boat, and
soon we had the hind aboard and were rowing merrily home.

The dog was right up in the bows, where she stayed the whole
way back, her nose resting by the stem, sniffing the wind. I wondered at the time whether John had told her to do this to trim the
boat, because the weight of the hind plus himself made it heavy aft.

Chapter Nine

In the spring of 1952 it did not appear as if we were ever going to get away to the sharks, for everything seemed to be going wrong. The engine was installed and the boat was afloat but we could not move for want of a propeller and shaft, the excuse being that there was a shortage of brass in the country. To add insult to injury, the Norwegians were actually in Mallaig and all my efforts to get even a second-hand propeller and shaft proved of no avail. Eventually, with the season well started, the company who had made the engine produced a new set of stern-gear. In feverish haste we rigged it up and with the carpenter and engineer aboard we set off on a trial run.

During that first run the engine controls were not led to the wheelhouse and the engineer was in the engine room fiddling with a rev.-counter to see what she developed. When he opened her full out her head lifted out of the water and sea began to come in over her stern, but she certainly shifted. As a result of that trial run Johnny and I were forced to shift the ballast, putting most of it as far into her nose as we could until, when lying at rest, she was down by the head.

The very next morning we were away, full speed for Canna, but this time both Johnny and I looked forward to meeting the Norwegians. Although we caught plenty of sharks, we met no Norwegians until the following week. One evening just about dark we were lying at Canna pier when a Norwegian boat that I knew quite well steamed in and made straight for us. When we saw that she was coming to the pier, we slacked our ropes to allow her to lie alongside it and we, being the smaller boat, took the outside. Early next morning both boats prepared for sea and set off together, Johnny sitting at our stem shouting up to her skipper on the bridge. We left the harbour abreast steaming slowly into the calm sea and, having ascertained from Johnny where we were making for, the Norwegian prepared to take leave of us saying that he would see us there. Shouting 'Cheerio', he waved and increased his speed; waving back, I raised the throttle slightly, and so it went on, shouting and waving until the funnel that stuck out through the top of his wheelhouse was being all but shaken off the boat with the vibration, and still the two boats were abreast. By now his whole crew was lining the rail and we had reached our destination. The Norwegian was the first to ease down and, greatly intrigued by the performance, he bellowed at us to come alongside. Having spent the war here, the skipper had excellent English and as I drew alongside his first remark was: 'What the hell have you got down below there?'

I invited him to come aboard and look for himself, and, as the engine all but filled the little engine room, the crew came down in relays to examine our new and shining pride and joy.

Later on that day he had the laugh on us, for the first shark surfaced and we beat him to it, only to have it break our new three-and-a-half-inch rope at once, the first and only time this ever happened. It had come out of the coil in a snarl, and jammed in the roller, seconds after the harpoon was in the fish.

For the remainder of that season we held our own, being now faster than many of them, although some of the larger boats could still just beat us, but the *Traveller*, being smaller, was more easily manoeuvred. This frequently gave us the advantage and we more than made up for the débâcle of Boisdale Loch the year before.

On one memorable occasion Johnny and I had set off late on Monday for the other side of the Minch where the herring men had told me there were plenty of sharks. It was not a very nice day and we got quite a bashing before we got across. At last we gained the shelter of S Uist and steamed close under Uishnish Lighthouse, where there is plenty of water below the cliffs, so that we could brew up in calm water. On calm days when herring-fishing in the winter I had often been in there lying alongside the sheer wall of rock with its lighthouse perched on top of it, when the keepers, agile as monkeys, would scramble down to the boat for the herring we had indicated we had for them.

As it was by then too late in the day for sharkfishing, especially with a cold north wind blowing which would keep the sharks down, we decided to make for the 'Kettle', which is the local name given to a popular anchorage, much used by the herring fleet, just inside Loch Skiport and only three miles north of the light. On our way there we had to cross the mouth of a bight the fishermen call Shepherd's Bight, although I have never been able to discover why. As soon as we 'opened' this, I was greatly disappointed – as the fishermen had reported that there were no Norwegians in the area the previous week – to see fifteen of them lying at anchor up at the head of it, in three tiers, one astern of the other. I called Johnny up from below to have a look at the opposition we would have to compete with on the morrow, and as we could not, from this distance, recognize any of the boats we decided to go in among them and see if Jacob had returned from Norway. We gave the *Traveller* full throttle to make as brave a show as possible and swept through them with a fair turn of speed, our backwash making them all roll. We did not see the *Barmøy*, but the *Alvøy*, which we knew was there. Her skipper had given us a dram and several cigars apiece when last we had met, so we quickly slipped up alongside her to return the compliment, for as this was Monday our medicinal bottle was still full.

In the midst of this fleet of Norwegians the *Traveller* looked small and insignificant. At sea when there were no larger boats around to dwarf her she seemed big enough, but tied to the Norwegians she looked like a toy. On learning that we had not been fishing that day but had come straight from Mallaig, the *Alvøy*'s skipper invited us to his cabin for a dram. We said that we had come to ask him aboard our boat to try our Scotch whisky, but accepted his Schnapps just the same. I honestly believe that in the first place he came down aboard and into our little fo'c'sle against his will and it pleased me to see that the comfort we had achieved in such a confined space amazed him. It was a cold night, so we had a good fire going, and the tartan rugs covering our bunks on which we sat gave the place a dash of colour. There were a good number of books in a specially made bookshelf with hinged bars across so that they would stay put when we were at sea. On the starboard side just beyond the stove was the food locker and up in the forepeak below the gun-mounting was our wireless, surrounded by rubber shock-absorbers. We had a big-ship's porthole that let in a lot of light fitted into the deckhead and it could be opened when the atmosphere became too thick. The entire fo'c'sle, with the exception of the deckhead which was painted white, was cream, to make it as light as possible. There was a drawer below my bunk with places for glasses and bottles, arranged to keep them from smashing up when the weather was rough; I might add that it mostly accommodated jars of jam. He did not expect this comfort and told us so. We had noticed that the general run of fo'c'sles in the Norwegian boats, although perfectly adequate, lacked the finish of those of the Scottish ring-net fleet. We persuaded him to join us for dinner and Johnny produced from the oven a jigget of mutton with all the trimmings. On Mondays we usually had a really fine dinner as we had plenty of time to prepare it on our way out to the fishing grounds and Johnny had started preparing this even before there was shelter enough to get it cooking. He had roast potatoes, fresh green peas, and a bit of cauliflower to go with the mutton, and I had brought from home a jar of rowanberry jelly. I find the bitter tang of the latter to be the ideal accompaniment to roast mutton or venison and it greatly pleased the Norwegian. The second course was apple pie, a product of the Mallaig bakery, and we rounded off the meal with coffee and biscuits and a bit of Danish cheese.

Our air of cautious reserve diminished along with the whisky and soon we were swapping yarns as if we had known each other all our lives. The Norwegian frankly admitted that he had been a little dubious of coming aboard a Scotch shark-boat after all the fuss the newspapers had made. When our coffee pot was as empty as the whisky bottle, the Norwegian suggested that we should all climb back aboard the *Alvøy* for a nightcap before retiring, and anyway he wished us to sample his particular brand of coffee. So back aboard we went and aft to his cabin. Right off he produced a bottle, and taking out the cork flung it over the side, saying: 'We emptied your bottle, we'll empty this one now!'

Johnny does not normally drink at all, but rather than let the side down he drank a tot before begging to be excused, and off he went to his bunk, leaving me to sample the coffee the Norwegian was busily preparing. We had a couple of fried kippers and some bottles of beer before calling it a night and dawn was breaking when I left the *Alvøy*, not that it ever really gets dark up here in the summer.

I managed to climb down aboard the *Traveller* and was making my way carefully forward to the fo'c'sle hatch when, looking up towards the head of the bight, I saw the familiar black dorsal fin of a basking shark. I did not move for a second or two until I was certain that it really was a shark and not a mirage due to my having mixed my drinks; then I went quietly below to waken Johnny.

It took some persuasion to get him to go up on deck and see for himself. Then, on seeing the shark, he turned to me, whispering: 'SSSH! Don't wake up the Norwegians!'

As quietly as we could, we loaded old 'Sugan' and put all in order for a shot before I went aft to start the engine. As soon as it was running I climbed aboard the *Alvøy* and, hurrying aft to the skipper's cabin, threw open the door and shouted: 'Come on, get up! Are you going to sleep all day? The sharks are almost aboard your boat', before casting off our ropes and jumping down aboard the *Traveller*.

The shark was by now coming out of the bight to meet us, so we circled round in order to come up behind him. As the water was very clear, I had a good view of the whole fish, and when

Chapter Nine

Johnny fired saw that the harpoon had entered the back of its head. He turned and gave me the thumbs-up signal and thereby missed seeing the shark stop dead and, without so much as straightening out the rope, lie over on its side like a poleaxed bull. I jumped from the wheelhouse and got a hold of the harpoon rope, for I was almost certain that the shark was dead. I had seen this happen only once before, when, some years previously, I had hit a shark in the same place. We always argued about it; I imagine that if you are lucky enough to penetrate some vital part of the vertebra in this region you not only kill the shark outright but cut off the reflex action, like switching out a light. He was certainly dead, for we hauled him back to the boat hand over hand without having to use the winch. One might ask why we do not always aim for this same spot, and the reason is that it was difficult for us to retrieve our harpoon without losing a great deal of time once it was embedded in the cartilage. I have harpooned a number of sharks in the head, but only twice in my whole experience have I known a shark to be killed outright.

The noise of our gun reverberating around such an enclosed stretch of water was a rude awakening for the Norwegian sharkmen. It must have been very frustrating for them, as they emerged sleepily from their respective dens, to see us with a shark already alongside. Johnny and I did our best to appear oblivious of our audience, and were by now putting the wire on his tail, and in no hurry about it. It was our intention to tow the shark out beyond the Norwegian boats, where we would have more sea-room. By the time we were under way the Norwegian boats, still about 200 yards ahead of us, all had their engines running and I do not believe Shepherd's Bight had ever heard such a racket. They seemed to be in frantic haste to get up their anchors and several of them appeared to be loading their guns. It was only when a second shark broke surface, halfway between the Norwegians and us, that I realized the reason for all the excitement. They must have seen this second fish before we did, for we were fully occupied with the shark we were then towing.

The sight of this second fish made me open up the engine to full throttle, although the boat did not go much faster, for not only did the weight of the fish give us quite a list to port, but the drag as we towed him tail-first, hindered us considerably. At this juncture I noticed that one of the Norwegians was clear of the main group and was steaming full speed towards us. Johnny had not been idle; quickly sizing up the situation, he had jumped for his gunpowder tin and, using his cupped hand as a measure, had flung, rather than poured, the powder down the barrel and rammed home the wad with the harpoon shaft. I remember making a mental note of the amount of gunpowder that missed the barrel altogether. I do not believe a harpoon gun can ever have been loaded quicker than Johnny loaded his that morning, and yet to me, stuck in the wheelhouse, it seemed an age and I would have done anything to be able to help him; but if I had taken my hand off the tiller for a second, the drag on the port side would have put us right off course. At last he was ready and old 'Sugan' roared, to be instantly followed by the much sharper report of the Norwegian's gun. It was the proudest moment of my life when I saw our harpoon slam home, right into the fish just aft of its dorsal fin, and that the Norwegian harpoon had gone clean over the shark's back.

The question of what would have happened had both harpoons reached their mark at the same moment has often intrigued Johnny and me. We would have stood no chance in a tug of war but I had no intention of letting him take a fish from under my nose fifty yards from the shore with my harpoon already fast in it, for although I had taken no part in the newspaper agitation against the Norwegians that would have been adding insult to injury. On the other hand I had resolved that, if the Norwegian's harpoon had got home first, the fish would be justly his, and I would have cut my tackle and waited for him to hand me back my harpoon.

As we were in comparatively shallow water, the shark did not sound, but headed for the open sea. The speed at which we approached the shark allowed Johnny to pick up the harpoon rope and make it fast before we were off in a great swirl of foam, the shark towing us on towards the Norwegian fleet, now about 100 yards away. We had no control over the boat and I was quite certain that we must crash right in among them. The boat which had fired her harpoon sheered off at once and as we passed close by her the crew raised a great cheer. High up on her bridge I noticed her skipper, an old man with a white beard, snatch off his cap and wave it round and round his head like a schoolboy at a football match, cheering us on as we passed. In an effort to retard our progress I put our engine into full speed astern, but I might as well have asked the shark to slow down for all the difference it made. Lady Luck must have been on our side that morning, for the shark altered slightly to port; even so the boats on my starboard side had to split away from the main group, but as they were all under way they managed somehow to clear a channel for us. On we sped, right out through the fleet with the nearby crews shouting encouragement and ribald advice. The moment we were clear of the boats we gave the fish more rope, and Johnny and I danced round the deck hugging each other like a couple of French cabinet ministers.

Soon the Norwegians were out and circling round us, several of them coming in quite close to congratulate us. The sharker who had missed offered to help us, for he obviously thought that it would be difficult for so small a boat to handle two sharks at once. We refused the offer, as Johnny and I quite often worked two sharks when conditions were favourable. Had he been alone, we might have accepted, but the temptation to play to the gallery was too much for us when it became obvious that they were all going to sit there and watch. The fact that the boat was moving was no real hindrance to the removal of the liver from the first shark, a point that those of them who had already seen us in action should have appreciated, for, because of the pole, we had full control over our brailer, whereas their net buckets would have drifted away astern. Before we were clear of the second shark it had started to blow and the motion made it more difficult to get this liver aboard, in spite of the fact that we were no longer under way. As soon as we had the liver all safely in barrels, we cleared off north into Loch Carnan, having, we hoped, given our audience full value. There were fourteen barrels of liver in our hold before we had our breakfast.

Our success at sharkfishing aroused a great deal of interest among the ring-net fleet, for the sharkfishing season coincides with the slackest time of their year. Generally during the early summer months there is very little herring caught in the Minch area. At this time of year several ring-net boats tried the lobsters, while others went to the seine net. They reasoned that if I could make money at the sharks with the *Traveller*, then they ought to be able to do much better with their much faster and bigger boats. That year several ring-net men approached me and tried to persuade me to sell them our spare gun, but I would not play, for a spare gun at sea is worth its weight in gold, and my stock illustration of this was the story of the Pom at Pooltiel.

One day in Mallaig, Jim of the *Margaret Ann* drew me aside and asked me what I knew about the type of guns Watkins[1] had used, as he had been offered a couple of them. I explained that I had never been near enough to examine them and that any time I had seen Watkins's boats the guns had been securely buttoned up; nor had I myself seen Watkins catch a shark, although I had seen him trying. The guns, I thought, must be good enough as I believed that they were a small type of whaling gun which Norwegian fishermen used in the North Sea.

Some weeks later I met Jim again when he called me down aboard his boat to see the gear he had bought from Watkins. The guns were beauties, exactly the type I had expected. They were somewhat similar to the modern Norwegian gun that Harry Thompson had used during the last season the Soay Shark Co. had been in operation, with the difference that they were larger. They looked to be magnificent tools, but I remarked to Jim that of all

1 Anthony Watkins, a sharkfishing rival of Gavin Maxwell's.

the many Norwegian boats I had fished alongside I had never seen
any of them with this type of gun. The harpoons were made of
mild steel rod, less than an inch in diameter, and the warhead was
in the form of a roughly fashioned, four-sided solder bolt with a
pair of barbs of approximately five-eights mild steel rod on each
side. Doubtless they were excellent of their kind but when he
asked what I thought of them I told him that, in my opinion, they
were not man enough for their job. It seemed to me that if he got
into a big shark, the strain on the harpoon rope might bend the
barbs back like wire. The weight of a ring-net boat is roughly
three times that of the *Traveller* and her displacement would certainly be greater, thereby increasing proportionately the strain on
the harpoon rope when the fish began to tow. Nevertheless, Jim
fitted out three of his boats and away they went to try out their
gear. I did not meet them at sea during the first week of their
sharkfishing venture but that weekend, when all the boats were
home, Jim came up to Glasnacardoch in his car. He told me that
the harpoons had not been entirely successful. As I had anticipated, more than one had drawn out under the strain of an extra
big fish when the rope was put round the winch. I lent him about
twenty of mine which I hoped would see the three boats through
the season. Jim wanted to pay for them but we agreed in the end
that he should pay only for those he lost, returning the others at
the end of the year.

The next week we were working off Barra and one evening
while fishing among the ring-net fleet I met the *Golden Ray*, one
of the Manson ringers which had taken to sharkfishing. As the day
was calm, we strapped the two boats together and Johnny and I
went aboard to learn how they were getting on. We were pleased
to hear that they were just back from Mallaig where they had
landed a cargo of liver, the combined catch of two boats. Jim was
nowhere to be seen and, on inquiring where he was fishing, they
told us he had cleared off to the west side of Barra and out into
the open Atlantic on Monday morning and no one had seen hide
nor hair of him since.

I saw no more of the Mansons until the following Saturday when we were once again discharging our barrels of liver in Mallaig. The *Margaret Ann* came steaming into the harbour well down in the water, going all out with such a bone in her teeth that we saw at once that she was loaded to capacity. As she passed the *Traveller* to tie up ahead of us, Jim leant out of the wheelhouse and shouted: 'Come aboard here, Tex, and get these bloody harpoons you gave me! No more catching sharks for me – I've had enough of them.'

He later told me that failing to catch any sharks the first week had maddened him, and when I had given him some of my harpoons he had steamed away, well out to the west'ard and clear of the ring-net fleet, whose derisive laughter he had had to suffer the previous week. As Jim put it: 'I was determined to catch some, Tex, and in case there were any more failures I got away out of sight of the fleet. But I wish you had been with us for the sharks were as thick as flies about ten miles west of Barra Head Light.' His only audience had been a Norwegian sharker, whose success was equal to his own.

Jim did not stay at the sharks much longer, but I am sure that if he had he would have been the best of them all. A herring-man at heart, the mess the liver and blood had made of his lovely new, varnished boat, not to mention the scars and scratches the harpoons had left on her hull, displeased him. Not least of his objections was the butchery involved, which had caused him on several occasions to refer to Johnny and I as 'those pair of blood-thirsty baskets!' and the sharks as 'poor, innocent beasts', despite the fact that they must in their day have cost him hundreds of pounds in nets.

His brother, 'Willum John', who had been the chief instigator of the Manson shark enterprise, continued even into the following season, and caught a tremendous number of sharks. Later that year he acquired yet another gun, this time direct from Norway, and with it a number of Norwegian harpoons similar to the *Barmøy*'s, and as these fitted all the Manson guns they returned all the gear I had lent them. It is unfortunate that they did not start at least a couple of seasons before they did, for that year our fine price of £48 a ton for the raw liver dropped suddenly to £25 and a couple of weeks later fell to £15.

In an effort to justify the expenditure of fitting out, the Manson boats contracted to bring in the carcases. Once only had Johnny and I been persuaded to do this and we swore then: 'Never again!' Quite a number of people have expressed their astonishment at what appears to them to be an appalling waste. In the first place, they do not appreciate the weights involved, and secondly the physical characteristics of a shark, which include an excellent dermal armour. Instead of the normal flat scales of a bony fish, the cartilaginous shark has dermal denticles, and in Maxwell's day when we were cutting up sharks on the beach everyone's hands soon became sore and swollen, with the tips of the fingers and other parts of the hand which were in contact with the shark completely devoid of skin. To counteract this Maxwell produced what I can best describe as armourplated leather gauntlets, which I for one found it impossible to work in. Thirdly, from an economic point of view the return for the work involved was in many cases non-existent, when the shark had to be towed some distance to a beach and, as Maxwell has so aptly put it: 'the liver was the elephant's ivory', and as he further added: 'I failed completely, however, to convince my co-directors of the wisdom of this.' It is not surprising that the ordinary layman, too, labours under this misconception.

The reason for the sudden and, on our part, unexpected drop in the price of shark-oil, we understood to be the result of the world's whaling fleet getting back into its stride after the war. During the war years the Antarctic had had a rest from the attentions of the whalemen and by the end of the war the whale catchers were scattered to the ends of the earth; and in addition, a great number of them had been lost while acting as mine-sweepers. With edible oil at a premium, Maxwell's sharkfishing venture had hit the market at the right time and up until 1952 we had continued to enjoy a reasonable return on all sharks caught, but in the few years since the inception of sharkfishing as a profitable venture, the whaling fleet had gradually returned to normal. Spurred on by a war, science had made great strides in the art of destruction, so that with new boats and up-to-date gear the whaling industry was once again on top of its form. Their colossal catches had flooded the markets and, in accordance with the law of supply and demand, had brought about the inevitable drop in price. The Manson boats very soon found, just as we had, that dealing with the whole shark was an uneconomic proposition, although the sight of two cranes working in unison to lift a pair of thirty-foot fish one after another cautiously into a railway wagon on the pier head, whence the heads and tails protruded over the ends like the remnants of some lunatic Mardi Gras celebration, certainly provided the thrill of a lifetime for the holiday-makers in Mallaig.

This act was Jim Manson's grand finale before handing me back my harpoons, his last words on the subject being: 'If they want sharks, they can cut them up themselves!' We were both sorry that we could not follow their progress and see the reaction of the lorry drivers who met them at the other end.

Chapter Ten

Glad as Jeanne and I had been to go to Glasnacardoch, we could but view it as a temporary arrangement and both of us looked forward to the day when we would have a house of our own. We continued to be strongly attracted to Soay and I seldom passed it, making a practice of spending the night in Soay harbour where another boat would have made for Canna. On such a night in 1951 Johnny and I, having anchored the *Traveller* in the north harbour, met the island's ferryman. We were on our way to visit Sandy but stopped for a yarn and in the course of conversation I remarked that I might be back as his neighbour yet. I went on to tell him that Jeanne was in touch with Lord Malcolm Douglas Hamilton, at that time MP for Inverness-shire (Lord Malcolm and his brother the duke had been directors of the defunct Soay Shark Company) and that we hoped to take over the tenancy of either one of the island's two vacant crofts. This seemed to amuse Neil greatly.

'Why not offer for the island? I hear it's for sale,' he suggested with a grin as we parted.

Lord Malcolm very soon put Jeanne in touch with his brother's factor in Uist. This man had only recently been appointed factor to the Hamilton and Kinneil Estates in North Uist and, since the liquidation of the Island of Soay Shark Fisheries Limited, Soay had been handed to him for administrative purposes. There was a rumour current at that time that the islanders were petitioning for evacuation, as they could no longer make a living under present conditions. Their complaint was that the existing service of two boats a week was not frequent enough and they demanded a thrice-weekly service or removal to a better-served area. The nine crofting households, twenty-seven souls in all, although enjoying agricultural benefits to the extent of controlled rents, subsidised rates, grants and loans as available, and farmstock subsidies, could contribute little to the national larder. The cost of maintaining the Post Office and its radio link, the existing bi-weekly mail service, and the monthly visits (on different days naturally) of the doctor, the telephone linesman and the Welfare Officer from the National Assistance Board, who each had to hire a boat (from Soay) to take them to and from the island, must have been quite surprising. Perhaps someone in authority called for the figures and decided that the expenditure of a lump sum would be cheaper in the end than such a constant drain on public funds.

It was not, however, until much later that Jeanne and I knew anything of this; we thought of Soay simply as the delightful island, which it is without its attendant trail of trials and tribulations.

The following weekend when I got home I mentioned my conversation with Neil, after which I thought no more about it until some weeks later when, once again home from the sea, I found Jeanne strangely exuberant. It transpired that she had bought the island of Soay with possession as from November. Carried away by her own enthusiasm, it had not occurred to her until the deal was on the point of completion that I had yet to be consulted, and she was now a little dubious as to my reactions. Certainly my first thought was, why an island when we want a house? However, I did not then immediately appreciate that Jeanne as proprietrix would be in a position to buy out an absentee tenant at an agreed valuation.

It was not until March 1952, when we received a visit from three representatives of the Scottish Office who had been sent up to investigate the position on Soay, that we learned that the petition for evacuation was no rumour. At least two of the party were unable to hide their consternation when they heard that we intended to move to Soay as soon as we could. They put forward all sorts of arguments in an effort to dissuade us, stating most emphatically that, when the crofters left, the steamer service would be cut off and the radio link removed. I pointed out that, like thousands of other ex-servicemen, I had been trying for years to find a home for my family, but that the government had never offered me a house and croft with the cost of our moving paid out of public funds. As for the steamer service, I told them the old story of Clan MacLean's antiquity. A neighbouring chief had boasted to MacLean of having had an ancestor in the Ark, but I, like the MacLeans, had a boat of my own.

They were far from pleased at our determination, for, as successive governments are for ever making a great song and dance about repopulating the Highlands and Islands, evacuation was a direct reversal of policy, and one which would be difficult to vindicate if we succeeded in spite of the lack of amenities enjoyed by the people they intended to move.

There was on Soay an empty cottage belonging to the estate. It was of similar design to the crofters' cottages, with two main bedrooms upstairs and two rooms downstairs. Mr William Meikle, the last tenant landlord, had completely rebuilt it and since his departure during the '14–'18 War it had become the custom for itinerant missionaries to be housed there while staying on the island, using the adjoining barn, which Mr Meikle had re-roofed and completely lined, in which to hold their meetings. When it became definite that the crofters were to be moved to Mull in the spring of 1953, we inquired of the Free Church of Scotland if there was any likelihood of a missionary being appointed before they left. On learning that no missionary was to be appointed, we decided to move into this cottage. At the same time we offered to put up any visiting missionary and to accord every facility for worship. To this suggestion the Free Church readily agreed and they did in fact send over two missionaries on separate occasions, who held services in Gaelic which I attended, before the ultimate departure of the crofters.

One rainy day during the 1952 sharkfishing season Johnny and I, finding ourselves on Soay, took the opportunity to look over the cottage. It was not in such good repair as its outside appearance suggested. We found that some of the inside doors did not fit; they obviously did not belong to the house for they were made of roughly sawn boards. The tiny kitchen range had, to put it kindly, seen better days. There was no water supply, although there were the remains of one in evidence. The small centre bedroom upstairs had been a bathroom, but was now minus the usual fittings; all that remained were the ugly, hacked-off ends of the lead pipes, now stuffed with paper to exclude the draughts. The varnish on the once bright walls was dark and cracked with age, and further marred by dismal streaks of peat stain. In accordance with the old Highland custom, the windows were minute, and what feeble rays of light succeeded in penetrating the lush greenery around them were quickly engulfed by the all-pervading gloom. The bedrooms sagged with layer upon layer of thick and gummy wall-paper; the master bedroom boasted a broken bogey stove, stuck well out into the room, with which some previous occupant had replaced a mislaid fireplace, hiding the gaping hole in the wall with a sheet of tin through which he had poked the bogey's funnel.

The only storage space I could see in the entire cottage was a tiny cupboard under the stairs; not even a shelf in the kitchen on which to put a pot. This lack probably accounted for the extraor-dinary number of assorted nails which studded the kitchen walls and on which we both ripped our oilskins, for, brown with rust, they lurked wonderfully camouflaged against the varnish. On opening the cupboard door we found the remnants of an aged spinning-wheel, a basket containing the string off years of parcels, and, curiouser and curiouser, a truly enormous cardboard box crammed full of empty gin bottles. It was obvious that a tremen-dous amount of renovation would have to be done and that I alone would have to take the place of the army of Mistress Mops that would have been employed to remove the grime of years if the cottage had not been on an island. Jeanne had promised Lady

Katherine that she would remain at Glasnacardoch until September before we finally departed for Soay.

With the price of shark-liver so low, Johnny and I stopped early that year. Towards the end of July when the fish started to go north we put our gear ashore, and Johnny went to work in a deer forest while I began moving our furniture. Taking over a small cargo in the *Traveller* on Monday mornings, I spent the remainder of the week working at the cottage. Without the *Traveller*'s mast and derrick many of the larger pieces would have been impossible to get aboard my little coble, which I was forced to carry back and forth with me. Getting ashore double beds, wardrobes, etc., was quite a business, for on arrival in Soay Bay I anchored the *Traveller* as close to the house as possible, launched the coble and lashed it fore and aft alongside. With the aid of my winch and derrick I lifted a large piece of furniture and lowered it gently down, before jumping in myself to get it into position with enough room to row. Then away I would go with the wardrobe or double divan bed precariously balanced across the ten-foot-long boat. This brought to mind the story of the efficiency expert whose imperious notices to 'THINK!' were posted in prominent positions round one of the London Film Studios. His progress was closely followed by a wit from the Art Department who added the cogent afterpiece 'OR THWIM!' The heaviest item of all was the Aga cooker which was to replace the useless little range in the kitchen. The only possible way to get it aboard the *Traveller*, let alone off-load it at Soay, was to take it apart, and I was lucky that on this occasion I had Johnny with me, because the islanders' way of expressing their disapproval at what I imagine they considered my temerity in electing to live where they had failed, was to remain invisible while I was at work, with the exception of Ronald of the *Hetty* who was, unfortunately, not always on hand. To have appeared without offering assistance would have been a contravention of their own code.

The Aga made a tremendous difference to the cottage and enabled me to have a constant supply of boiling water on hand in a series of kettles. There was a small stream close by which had served the needs of the cottage since the disappearance of the piped water. I rolled up my sleeves and, armed with a scrubbing brush, a scraper and an enormous carton of sugar soap, I stripped the walls right down to the bare wood before re-varnishing them. The finished effect of the bedrooms was reminiscent of a ship's cabin. Unless we were prepared to have the front door ever open, it was impossible to see anything at all in the hall, where not only was the varnish black with age, but all the doors were painted a drab chocolate colour. To overcome this I fitted a large brass port-hole into the front door and this, together with a brass replica of a sailing vessel, which was to serve as a door-knocker, gave it a pleasantly nautical air.

Chapter Eleven

While I was working at the house the three government officials who had reported on the situation, and who were ultimately to arrange the evacuation, again visited Soay. Their purpose was to hold a meeting of the crofters at which they laid before them their proposals for the solution of the island's problems. Not unnaturally I wished to attend to hear at first hand what these proposals were, and was greatly surprised when I was turned away along with two visitors. In fact I never did get in to any of the meetings held by the Scottish Office with the Soay crofters. I later learned that the people were given the choice of being moved to one of several government estates belonging either to the Department of Agriculture for Scotland or the Forestry Commission. Throughout this meeting I understood the word 'evacuation' was not used by the officials. At yet a third meeting it was finally settled that the crofters were to move to the island of Mull. There the Department had acquired a large house and were to turn it into flatlets for the Soay people. The Press, ever hungry for a juicy morsel, seized upon this, flocked to the island, and even invaded Glasnacardoch to pester Jeanne and me with their questions. The resultant newspaper reports were fantastic, for the lovely little isle of Soay was transformed overnight into a 'barren splinter of the Hebrides', a 'rock to which the unfortunate inhabitants had to carry the soil upon their backs' in order to grow a potato, and separated from Skye not by the beautiful Soay Sound, but by a 'mile of water over which some evil spirit brooded'. Such is the power of the Press.

I had made the Soay cottage habitable some time before the second week of September, when Jeanne was free to leave Glasnacardoch. By then I had moved all our furniture with the exception of the camp beds in which we slept during the last few days. Nevertheless, when the great day dawned, there still remained an amazing collection of small things to be stowed in some sort of container. To add to our frustration, we could not get a lorry to bring the last of our stuff down to Mallaig pier until six p.m. and it was after seven before we were aboard the *Traveller* and under way.

There was a cold north wind blowing, so all three of us crammed into the wheelhouse to get the benefit of the heat from the engine. On rounding Sleat Point we encountered nasty, choppy seas which we luckily could meet head-on all the way to Soay. The sudden alteration in the motion of the boat made me keep an eye on Duncan, for I did not know how he would react. I need not have worried; he began to sing, or rather to make singing noises, which he kept up all the way.

We reached Soay in a little over two hours and, as it was long past Duncan's bedtime, we decided to leave all the stuff aboard the boat until morning, but he flatly refused to leave the boat unless his tricycle was brought ashore with him. He was never able to use it, but for a day or two he carted it about bodily from place to place looking for a road on which to ride it, until the foreshore, with all its fascinating rock-pools peopled by creatures that swam or crawled or wriggled, claimed his attention. It has remained his playground and through time his knowledge of its inhabitants has become surprisingly wide. He is an expert and ardent beach-comber and, where some small boys collect trains or model cars, Duncan collects unusual shells, only too often still occupied by their original owners, until now his bedroom resembles a corner of the Natural History Museum, complete with whale's vertebrae and smelly things in jars. Sea-urchins hold first place, but he has to be forcibly reminded that we prefer to have only the shell in the house, and he has yet to appreciate Emerson's lines:

Chapter Eleven

I wiped away the weeds and foam,
I fetched my seaborne treasures home,
But the poor, unsightly, noisome things,
Had left their beauty on the shore,
With the sun and the sand and the wild uproar.

Ronald of the *Hetty* had stoked up the Aga and lit the lamps for us, so the cottage was bright and warm when we arrived. Like a true West Highlander he had the kettle boiling before we were ashore. All the Soay houses used paraffin lighting, mostly Tilley pressure lamps. These give an excellent light, but I found the hissing noise they make disconcerting. I never notice it now, nor would I have any other form of lighting on an Hebridean island, for these lamps perform the double function of lighting and heating a room. I must admit that when I came to live on Soay first I often, on entering a room in the dark, felt for the electric-light switch, and Jeanne sometimes does this yet.

The small centre room upstairs was to be Duncan's bedroom and he had been looking forward to having his big, grown-up bed, a new single divan which we had promised he would have on Soay. When he was shown his new bedroom for the first time, the look of joy on the child's face was as good as a tonic to me. Inside were all the lost toys that he had imagined gone for ever when I had spirited them off in the night with the furniture. He rushed in and picked up this and that, but settled for his teddy-bear and, refusing to be separated from it, went to sleep with it tucked in beside him.

The year was now too old to plant any vegetables for use during the coming winter and in any case the garden was waist-high with ragwort, nettles and docks. The only thing I could do was scythe them down to prevent them re-seeding. As the crofters were still busy haymaking, and as we had bought in Mull a couple of pedigreed dairy goats to ensure a supply of tuberculin-free milk for Duncan, I took lessons in the art of scything. The hay we made in all the odd corners we took home to the goatshed in huge bundles on the coble when the wind was favourable; otherwise I would never have been able to row at all, for the huge floating haystack was a formidable sail.

The most sensible way to get the goats to Soay was for me to go and collect them myself. The roundabout journey by steamer, road and rail transport that they would otherwise have to take in order to reach the island was obviously not desirable, for, quite apart from the expense, it would not have been kind to the animals.

One fine morning about the beginning of October we set off in the *Traveller* for Tobermory in Mull, where the goats would be awaiting our arrival. Donald, brother of Ronald of the *Hetty*, went with me. We set our course for the east side of Eigg, and were not long out of Soay when the wind began to freshen from the west, and the *Traveller* was soon showering herself with spray at every dive. By the time we had gained the shelter of Eigg it was blowing half a gale and raining very heavily. There was certainly too much wind for us to attempt to round Ardnamurchan, the most westerly point of the Scottish mainland, a place one is well advised to keep clear of with contrary winds. Donald was in no hurry to return to Soay, so we decided to run for Eigg Harbour which, with westerly wind, is safe enough, but I remarked to Donald, on our way in, that nothing would persuade me to enter it if the wind was southerly, after the carry-on I had had the last time, and we came into the anchorage very cautiously. After we had dropped the anchor, we made ourselves comfortable for the night, for even although it was still quite early neither of us had any wish to go ashore.

We awoke next morning to brilliant sunshine, with only a light breeze of southerly wind blowing, so as soon as we had had a cup of tea we set off. It was a pleasantly uneventful journey down and on arrival in Tobermory we contacted the lady with whom the goats had been left. She immediately brought us to them and we were most amused to see them chase her dog for its life when it approached too close. The milking goat was tall, almost as large as a hind, and every bit as stately, very much the duchess with her slightly Roman nose. She was biscuit-coloured, with the white facial markings of the Swiss goats; the kid was obviously a different strain, white with a cheeky, dished face, and shorter, thicker legs. Both were hornless, one being polled and the kid having been disbudded in infancy. Such were Nina and Blondie, or according to their herd-book entries, Buttersea Karenina and Fionn Blondie, Nina being a much travelled goat from the Fen country, while Blondie was born and bred in Mull. They quickly demonstrated two outstanding capric characteristics, curiosity and friendliness, for they made no bones about coming with me, and trotted willingly down the road to the pier, where there was no difficulty in getting them aboard the boat and down into the hold.

We wasted very little time in Tobermory, for we felt that, once the goats were aboard the boat, we must keep going, as it would never do to get storm-struck *en route* with a couple of goats to feed. As soon as possible we were away, full speed, up the Sound of Mull towards Ardnamurchan. On rounding it we found that what had been a light breeze of southerly wind in the morning was now a fairly strong one, and with much more west in it. I was a bit worried as to how the goats would react, but found that they were cudding happily, oblivious of the tossing we were getting. The weather did not improve, and by the time we reached the shelter of Eigg we had to pump quite a lot of water out of the *Traveller*, for I had removed the after-hatch cover so that the goats could get plenty of fresh air. Even I find the fumes from a diesel engine particularly offensive, and the bilges of most fishing boats fairly 'snoosht' when they are disturbed. The goats had kept dry and were only too willing to eat the hay I offered them when I went down at Eigg to see how things were. It was now almost dark and, as the wind had increased, we eased down the engine and lit our Primus, so that we could have some tea in the shelter afforded by the bulk of Eigg.

We soon had a mug of tea and a sandwich apiece, if you can call it a sandwich, for I fried half a dozen sausages and some ham and presented Donald with two whole slices of bread with three sausages and a couple of slices of ham between them. As soon as we had finished this, we made off full speed again, on the last lap of our journey.

I was down below with the goats, trying to get them to go as far forward in the hold as possible, where they would remain dry. I knew that when we left the shelter behind us we would 'whistle some' before we got across the sound of Rum. Experience has taught me that when the wind has west in it there is invariably a heavy sea running through there, but I did not expect to encounter seas such as those which met us the moment we opened the sound. The first one struck her clean on the broadside, flinging her right over on her beam ends; the suddenness of this sent the two goats and me spinning, to land in a heap on the starboard side of the hold, only to be instantaneously flung across to the other side. Donald, experienced seaman and all as he is, was caught napping, and I could feel that he was fighting to bring her head up to meet the sea, but he was not in time, for yet another sea caught us on the broadside, this time breaking on deck and pouring down into the hold. I got the full benefit of this as I was halfway out of the hatch, making for after to take the tiller; unfortunately the goats, which had hitherto kept dry, got their share of this and I saw the kid swept clean off its feet by the amount of water that went down. The next wave we met stem-on and the *Traveller* rode it well, but Donald was too late in easing the engine down and we fell into the trough on the other side of the wave with a tremendous wallop, added to which was an ear-splitting screech from the engine room, as if a thousand devils had caught their tails in the flywheel. I shut the throttle right down to dead slow, nipped below to see the reason for the racket, and was horrified to find that the fuel tank had broken loose and was now lying on the engine-room floor. The fearful din we were hearing was caused by the friction set up when it came into violent contact with the flywheel every time the boat rolled. This would quickly wear a hole in the tank, but there was very little I could do about it, for I certainly could not lift it. I figured that there were at least sixty gallons of fuel in it and, so long as the feed pipes were not broken and the level of fuel in the tank remained higher than the fuel pump; all would be well. I got a rope round the fore-end of the tank, and somehow managed to heave it clear of the flywheel, and it was only then that I noticed that the feed pipe was spurting oil like a cut artery. It was broken more than half through, joined only by a thread. For just such an emergency I carried aboard a length of Calor-gas tubing and, cutting a six-inch piece, I quickly snapped the thread that held the pipe and thrust both ends into this tube, to make a perfect joint. The fact that we were going so slow enabled me to do this, for the unusually large fuel filter with which the *Traveller* is fitted retained sufficient oil to keep the engine running. As soon as I could, I appeared on deck and told Donald what went on below, and suggested to him that we should make full speed for Rum, in the shelter of which we could fix things up better, and I stayed below all the way there in case the tank should break loose again.

The *Traveller* remained on her best behaviour and soon we were in the calm of Loch Scresort in Rum, where we made for the pier and stopped the engine. I went immediately to see if the goats had survived their passage so far, and was pleased to see them lying down together contentedly. Before we made any attempt to rectify things in the engine room I suggested a cup of tea, but, on entering the fo'c'sle to light the Primus, I got the shock of my life, for the mess that met me would have to be seen to be believed. The cooking stove, of which I was so proud, was smashed to pieces and was now so many filthy bits of rusty iron, scattered all over the place, even on my bunk. The door of the grub locker had burst open, and the tin of milk we had been using had, by now, gone a long way towards repainting the fo'c'sle. Jam had added its dash of red here and there, mostly on the floor, but soot from the smashed stove predominated. Luckily we had not lit the fire that day, but had used the Primus when preparing our food.

We siphoned about ten gallons of fuel out of the main tank, before lashing it securely away from the flywheel, and rigged up a small two-gallon tank, which had been the petrol tank when the

Traveller had the petrol/paraffin engine. This was connected up to the fuel pump and it was our intention to fill it periodically by means of an old teapot which I kept for putting oil in the crank-case. After we had had our tea we started her up again and were soon steaming full speed for Soay. All went well, and on arrival Ronald came out to meet us with my coble, and ferried us ashore, goats and all, in one go. Jeanne was waiting on the beach as we landed, and quickly brought the goats up to the little stone building at the head of the beach, just below the house. It was built by Mr Meikle as a kennel for his gun-dogs, and since then had been used as an engineer's workshop, a bachelor home for two fishermen, and a byre for a missionary's cow. It is now known as the goatshed.

I was promptly ignored, or at least left to fend for myself, while the goats were given every attention, rubbed down, given hot drinks with salt in, and a basinful of dairy nuts apiece. I invited Donald to join us for dinner, if there was any to be had with all this excitement over a couple of goats. When eventually Jeanne did appear, she had the audacity to inquire what had kept us on such a fine night, for the village bay in Soay is beautifully sheltered from the west wind. She refused to believe us when we explained that there was a gale blowing outside, but changed her tune when I emptied out my rubber boots on her nice clean kitchen floor.

As the winter advanced it became increasingly obvious that one of our prime needs was a piped water supply. We both tried to dodge the never-ending chore of carrying water from the nearby burn; it seemed incredible that the three of us could use so much. Many a wet and stormy night did I have to leave the comfort of a chair by the fire, put on boots and oilskins, and dash for a bucket of water, before I could have a cup of coffee. The cost of bringing out tradesmen to an island is prohibitive, so we set about bringing the water to the house ourselves. To ensure a constant supply I built a concrete tank on the hill above the house to trap the burn higher up. Between the house and the tank there was an impenetrable thicket of birch and alder scrub laced together with brambles. No doubt it had been cherished by our predecessors, the island's transient missionaries, as a formidable barricade against the cattle which were allowed into the township in winter. On hacking our way into this thicket while laying the water pipes we found that it had other uses. It had formed a handy answer to the islanders' philosophy 'out of sight, out of mind' where rubbish was concerned. Here we found an incredible miscellanea, old bully-beef tins, broken bottles, bed ends, and a perfectly good Primus stove. Duncan's treasure was an old wireless from which he removed many of the component parts to build an engine for his boat, so he said.

To bring water to the house was one thing, but getting it out again was another. The renovation of what remained of the old waste pipes entailed the digging up of the lot. The few serviceable ones we cleaned out and used again, when we laid a complete wastepipe from the kitchen, under the path at the back of the house, right through the garden and on down the beach to low-water mark. I installed a sink at a height Jeanne had indicated, for, being tall, she had yet to find a kitchen sink that she did not have to stoop over. The installation of running water in a house is a very commonplace thing, but to us it seemed a wonderful achievement. When the tap was first turned on at the opening ceremony, anyone seeing our hilarity might have wondered if we had struck oil.

We were not long settled in when the island received yet another visit from officialdom in the person of a single member of the original trio. He did not hold a meeting, but went from house to house and was gone almost before we knew that he had come, for he did not call on us. We concluded his visit had to do with the forthcoming evacuation and thought no more about it. However, next mail day when I called at the Post Office to collect our mail, I was presented with eight registered letters post-marked 'Soay'. It might not have seemed quite so odd had I not been standing shoulder-to-shoulder with the senders, most of whom passed my door several times a day on their way to and from the north harbour. At this point the footpath is so narrow that, were I to stand in the middle of it, I could touch my front door with one hand and the fence on the opposite side of the path with the other.

On opening the first letter, we found it to contain a formal renunciation of the writer's holding on Soay. A moment's comparison assured us that all eight were identical; our friend from the Scottish Office had done his work well and ensured that there would be no hitch in the Secretary of State's plans. Within a short time the renunciations were followed by a further sheaf of registered letters, this time from the Scottish Land Court in Edinburgh, containing an equal number of claims for compensation, which together amounted to a bill for over £3,800. The picture now began to emerge, for we had already received the following letter (quoted in full):

Department of Agriculture for Scotland,
St Andrew's House,
EDINBURGH 1.
29th October, 1952.

115406/2

Dear Sir,

Soay Island

With reference to previous correspondence, I am writing to let you know that the Department are in process of completing an agreement for the acquisition of Craignure House and lands, Island of Mull, where as you are no doubt aware it is proposed to resettle the people who wish to leave the Island of Soay.

The Department are now writing to each of the tenants of Soay offering them accommodation in Mull. This new accommodation will be available for occupation by Martinmas 1953, but it may be practicable to settle some, if not all, of the tenants there before that date.

Yours faithfully,

(Signed) Secretary.

Chapter Eleven

It was clear that the Secretary of State, having decided upon the expenditure of a lump sum, had no intention of making it a forced evacuation. At the same time he did not make it easy for us to meet our liabilities in the normal way. Having once 'resettled' the Soay tenants, and after all services to the island had been withdrawn, he doubtless reasoned (if bureaucrats do reason) that no new tenants would come forward to repeople it. When a crofter renounces his holding the landlord must pay him the value of all buildings and any other works which the Land Court see fit to call improvements suitable for an agricultural holding, at a value agreed between parties, or fixed by them, which he can then reclaim in full from the incoming tenant who takes over the holding. Who would pay this compensation? I was certainly not in a position to pay it, and had I been given an opportunity I would have said so.

In the early spring the forthcoming visit of the Land Court was heralded by an outburst of furious activity on the part of the islanders. Ugly rusty iron roofs were hastily tarred to hide the neglect of years, their jagged edges snipped off and minute new pieces cunningly slipped underneath. Whitewash brushes, pots of paint and lots of elbow grease were used inside and out, until the houses shone with solidarity and virtue, their woodworm camouflaged, their leaks stopped up with pitch.

Conditions in crofting areas and the complex body of law which has grown up to govern them since 1886, when the first Crofting Act was passed, have resulted in the formation of a body known as the Scottish Land Court to interpret them, to arbitrate and to evaluate. The members are appointed by the Secretary of State for Scotland who, nevertheless, is himself subject to decrees enacted by them. The Court includes not only lawyers and surveyors but men of wide experience and first-hand knowledge of crofting conditions. There must always be a Gaelic-speaking member, for, although there are very few Gaelic speakers who are not bilingual, there must be many, particularly among the older generation, who can express their thoughts most clearly in their native tongue. When a dispute involves valuations or boundaries and like questions, the Court is held on the spot. The improvements on a holding are legally the property of the proprietor, which he hands on from tenant to tenant with appropriate changes in valuation according to whether their condition has been bettered or allowed to deteriorate, and it is this question that the Land Court must often be called upon to arbitrate.

Never before having had any dealings with this Court, the title then conjured up a picture of a body of essentially legal gentlemen, and it was with not a little surprise that we were introduced to the two tweed-clad Highland gentlemen who were to constitute the Court on Soay. The senior, the Gaelic-speaking member, was to do the valuations and the other was a lawyer.

We all assembled in the schoolroom, the chairman taking his place in the teacher's desk while the rest of us crammed into the children's desks, which were designed for the ages of five to twelve. I found myself in one of the former and spent an acutely uncomfortable session with my knees drawn up to my chin.

The proceedings opened with the crofters being asked to describe their holdings and to list again the improvements for which they were claiming compensation. The question of how many cows each was allowed to keep caused a great deal of nattering in the wings, in Gaelic. I imagine the object of the question was to try and arrive quickly at a reasonable estimate of the arable part of the holding and thus its value, but the results were so confusing that the chairman went away on another tack with the question: 'How much can you plough?' put to each in turn.

I found the answers, which in some cases amounted to several acres, somewhat startling since I had never seen a plough, nor had I ever heard of one, on Soay. Nevertheless, the figures were faithfully written down to be recorded permanently in the archives of the Land Court.

The next two days were spent visiting each holding in turn, inspecting houses and barns, drains and ditches. Some claims included such grandiose items as 'clearing the stones from the

cultivated land', 'roads', and 'deep trenching', as well as 'walls –
value to be left to the discretion of the Land Court'. The first item
turned out to be a small walled garden, and the second, where
they could be identified at all, appeared as grassy tracks neatly
bordered with stones. The deep trenching was an admirable
example of a tank trap; it had been a peat cutting and now was
filled with black and oozy slime, a danger to man and beast. As for
the walls, they appeared to be the drystone ruins of the homes of
the claimant's ancestors, now no more than banks of mossy,
lichen-encrusted stones.

When they had heard all we had to say, inspected everything
and entered their comments in their little black books, the Court
departed, leaving us to ponder the results of their deliberations for
another month.

As the date of the evacuation was fixed as 19 June, 1953, the
departure of the Land Court in May saw yet another burst of
activity. Fences vanished overnight to make crates for hens, and
the boxes and bags bespoken from the Mallaig grocers began to
arrive. A projected move is an event for any family but to folk like
these it was an upheaval of the first magnitude. Coming of generations born and bred under the same roof, packing was an entirely
new experience, and one which required a great deal of thought,
more especially as every mortal thing would have to be manhandled down the beaches.

A few days before the evacuation date I went to Mallaig to pick
up Kenneth Allsop and Haywood Magee of *Picture Post* who had
arranged to stay with us throughout the operation. When I arrived
in Mallaig, I was mobbed by reporters, each one clamouring to get
to Soay ahead of the others, but the snag was where they were to
stay. *Picture Post* had stolen a march on them, for obviously none of
the crofters in the throes of moving could possibly put up any of
them. The following morning, and every morning as long as the
evacuation was in progress, the 'daily papers' arrived *en masse*, twenty
or thirty to a boat-load, to spend the rest of the day wandering

about, getting underfoot and halting laden crofters in midstride while they took pictures. Bobbing about among the crowd was the much more popular TV Newsreel man; a picture in the papers was becoming commonplace, but TV was definitely 'U'.

In the early hours of 16 June we awoke to find the SS *Hebrides* lying at anchor in the middle of the bay, her funnel belching black smoke as she kept up steam for her winches, which were soon working overtime. Steam-powered and fifty-five years old, she was the last of her class in the MacBrayne fleet. Some years previously this 750-ton ship had been taken off the passenger service and was now carrying mixed cargo around the Hebrides.

Every available pair of hands would be needed and, after I had eaten a hasty breakfast, I went off in the *Traveller* to Glen Brittle, where I picked up the farmer's sons and anyone else who was willing to come and lend a hand. By the time I got back, the reporters had arrived from Mallaig, the bay was filled with motor launches, and their parties of interested sightseers had disembarked to swell the milling throng on the beach. It was probably the largest and, I am sure, the noisiest, gathering that Soay Bay has ever seen.

Motor boats were chugging to and fro, their occupants shouting to each other above the noise of their engines. The human clamour ashore was often augmented by the hysterical barking of the island's bewildered dogs; perhaps they knew that there was no future for them in Mull. The dogs, having no resistance to the diseases of civilization, quickly fell victim to an epizootic which was probably hardpad. The dominating noise was the constant rattle of the *Hebrides'* winch as she hoisted the gear out of the laden boats alongside to be lowered down into one of her cavernous holds.

All the suitable boats on the island were pressed into service to ferry the bits and pieces out to the steamer from each household in turn. For the heavier things the islanders used a flat-bottomed salmon coble which could be run right onto the beaches.

The reporters' departure for the day was timed to get them back to Mallaig before closing time, but still the work went on well into the night. The next two days were equally chaotic and on the morning of the last day the *Hebrides* moved her station to just outside the north harbour to pick up the cattle. The cattle were gathered together in the village and driven in single file along the path and past my door to the shark factory at the harbour. The scene in the enclosure there was as good as any rodeo, for getting them into a boat required almost as many men as there were cattle. Each cattle beast had to be caught and hauled on to the minute wooden pier, where an enormous canvas sling was slipped below its belly. Maxwell's old hand crane was called into service, requiring much greasing and persuasion to perform at all; the handles were found, and each beast was heaved slowly off its feet to dangle precariously with much loss of dignity over the hold of the Mallaig launch *Islander*, whose job it was to ferry the cattle out to the waiting *Hebrides*.

With all the cattle aboard, the steamer returned to the village bay to collect the last of the islanders' gear and finally the people themselves, although it was almost dark before the last of them were safely embarked. The steamer was scheduled to leave Soay at midnight so that she would arrive in Mull early next morning, where a welcoming committee, including a representative of the Secretary of State and the local MP, would be waiting. The reporters therefore had time to dash to Mallaig, dispatch the late night news and, more important yet, lay in supplies for the journey. They also brought out an enormous bag of mail which was handed to the postmistress, now retired. Mail had been pouring over to the island all the week with the almost constant stream of boats from Mallaig. A great number of the letters were from collectors eager to get the Soay date stamp to mark an historic occasion. About eleven o'clock Jeanne, Duncan and I went out to make our farewells; by then spirits were high, for the *Mirror* had arrived back from Mallaig with the supplies – at least one case of whisky and several of beer. The ship was a blaze of lights and toasts of relief, farewell and regret were being drunk from the VIP cabins of the Scottish Office officials right down to the hold among the cattle, where the older men had gathered. Here Sandy had stationed himself and was doing his best to drown out the bellowing of the bemused beasts with renderings of ancient Highland airs on the bagpipes. To some of the younger people the whole operation was an enjoyable experience, for not only had it brought them into the public eye but it also promised them a new life in Mull. To have an entire steamer to themselves was the height of luxury and they were not troubled by the memories which haunted the older people who might never see Soay again. Certainly the stewards had laid on an excellent meal and were all set to make it a memorable trip, at the government's expense. In the saloon we received last-minute instructions about the hens and the cats which had taken to the hills at the critical moment. We had intended to remain aboard the steamer until she left, when we would have accompanied her out of the bay, but before long the wind freshened and as the *Traveller* was bumping badly against her steel side we could not wait.

On reaching the house we lit another lamp and had our supper, with one eye on the clock. Just before midnight the winches began to rattle for the last time as the *Hebrides* heaved in her anchors. At this Jeanne and I, each carrying a 300-candle-power Tilley lamp, went out and stood by the door so that the islanders' last view should not be of an island left in darkness.